The Myth of Enlightenment

The Myth of Enlightenment

Seeing Through the
Illusion of Separation

By Karl Renz

INNER DIRECTIONS®
The Spirit of Insight & Awakening

Inner Directions®

Inner Directions Foundation
P. O. Box 130070
Carlsbad, California 92013
Tel: 800 545-9118 • 760 599-4075
www.InnerDirections.org

Cover painting by Karl Renz
Cover and Interior design by Joan Greenblatt
Printed in Canada on recycled paper

ISBN-10: 1-878019-24-4
ISBN-13: 978-1-878019-24-0

Library of Congress Catalog Card Number: 2005929159

Acknowledgements

Original Editing in German by Dietmar Bittrich.
English Translation by Hans-Georg Turstig.
English Editing by Kevan Myers,
Ronald S. Miller, and Matthew Greenblatt.

"In the fleetingness of a shadow world, consciousness behaves actively and reactively. You're not part of the phenomena in the shadow world, but always prior to them. In reality nothing moves; there's only pure stillness."

Contents

Foreword

How Does Karl Renz
Get Away with It?

"No, thank you! I've had enough of Karl Renz!" I felt this after twenty minutes of listening to him speak. At the time, Christian Salvesen and I had visited several satsang teachers for our German book, *Die Erleuchteten Kommen* (*The Enlightened Ones Are Coming*). Near the end of our research, someone recommended Karl Renz, and we decided to include him in our book. After all, he did have an enlightenment experience. He had seen something that we hadn't, and he had a faithful audience in a number of cities.

On first contact, however, it seemed to me that this man was good for nothing. He talked too much and never, never kept still. He didn't spend time staring into your eyes, and he didn't create a spiritual atmosphere. He simply sat there like a seminar leader, without flowers, candles, photos of any gurus, or the slightest sign of spirituality.

Over the years I had participated in quite different satsangs. I had met teachers with magnetic auras; teachers who sat in silence with their eyes closed for a long time until the stillness spread throughout the entire room; teachers who looked deeply into your soul; "saints" who bestowed each word like a precious jewel. These teachers were surrounded by music, flowers, incense, and the images of great masters.

Karl Renz had none of the trappings of holiness. There were no prayers, no special atmosphere, nothing meditative at all. Even worse, his message was anti-meditative! I had meditated every morning and evening for 20 years. In one fell swoop, Karl declared that my discipline was simply futile! Whizz—it was gone! He continued in this vein as he critiqued time-honored spiritual approaches. Every path was an error, every effort futile, every search a hopeless case.

Many people in the audience enjoyed his iconoclastic message. Despite my initial critical assessment, by the end of the talk, I was high. I remained high as I drove home, and it continued even throughout the next day. It was as if I had received a small, illegal happiness pill during this talk, an injection of carelessness or a deeply effective means of relaxation. I felt that something must have had happened beyond all the talking, and to check out my theory I went again— and again. Now, as often as possible, I don't miss any talks when Karl comes to town.

I still think he talks too much; each session is two hours of a non-stop talk, interrupted only by questions from the audience. At the end of a session, he looks remarkably fresh and would love to continue, although the audience has had enough. People are generally worn out because everything they had thought about and believed in has been blown to the wind, every argument invalidated.

Karl Renz doesn't acknowledge any spiritual tradition or golden treasury of world wisdom. In his view, no knowledge discovered in deep realization can survive. Nothing! At the end of a talk, nothing is left. Whatever a seeker has thought or believed in is no longer valid. While this can be depressing, most of all it's a relief.

Some people who experience a shock-induced stiffness quickly get up at the end of the talk, never to come back again. Sometimes people leave in the middle of a talk, furiously silent or loudly argumentative. But, in general, most people have fun and laugh. The longer the talk lasts, the greater the laughter. Occasionally, there are laughing orgies, like children in kindergarten. In the beginning this got on my nerves quite a bit. If I dared to come forward with an honest question and the others burst into laughter, I reacted with irritation. Even now some of these silly things disturb me, especially when I find myself missing a joke.

But this is temporary because the real joke in Karl Renz's talks is that the one who feels disturbed disappears. The one who reacts with irritation is no longer there. Of course, the audience is still sitting on the same seats at the end, but by now they are beyond being disturbed. Whatever anybody thought he had to defend has vanished. That which constitutes a person (the so-called "identity") flutters away during the talk. The complex web of beliefs, experiences, and images that make up the self simply dissolves. One's ideas of how the world must be, along with how other people and oneself should be, disappear. Ideas of what should happen to bring one happiness become meaningless (even the idea that anything needs to happen at all). What remains in the end is often called "presence," a cheerful clarity that depends on nothing external.

If all this sounds good, you might wonder how Karl Renz is doing it. He maintains that he does nothing at all, and in a way this is true. The teacher who has realized his "true nature" is like a screen, not the movie projected on it; such a being is like the sky, not the clouds passing by. Knowing that he is stillness, such a teacher doesn't do anything. He is simply there without intention. However, his presence obviously has an effect, since it absorbs the restlessness of others. As Paul Brunton said about Ramana Maharshi, "He is an emptiness into which the thoughts of the others can fall."

Even though Karl is doing nothing, something profound goes on around him. That's why he is invited to so many countries. Each year, for his own joy, he spends part of the winter in the South Indian city of Tiruvannamalai. He spends hours each day talking to an international group of people, including those who have been searching for years through a succession of gurus and those who are just beginning. In his carefree, unique version of English, Karl gets into his stride, using a conversational style that involves turning serious inquiry into an occasion for humor.

He especially plays with words and their deeper meanings. He twists them, takes them apart, and juggles them; discovers a secondary and tertiary meaning; and arrives at enlightening points, quite often to his own surprise.

In addition, he certainly has a Socrates within him, which gives his art of verbal juggling its magical quality. Like the ancient Greek philosopher, he leads his audience, filled with intellectual questions and disputes, to a state of *aporia* (which is the friendly philosophical term for hopelessness).

In his conversations, Socrates showed people who believed they knew something that in truth they were ignorant. This is exactly what goes on with Karl. In the beginning, nearly everyone who comes to his talks believes that he knows something or has enough understanding to move a few steps on the path to enlightenment. Jokingly, yet relentlessly, Karl crushes people's reliance on beliefs and knowledge.

In the end, both questioner and audience are stripped of their concepts, without their being a winner or loser. Since all are one, the surrender that is the outcome of this exchange brings a relief to everyone, including the questioners. They discover that the mind itself creates the problems that it struggles to solve. They also see that the truth, the essence, the Self of everyone is prior to the mind. While the mind can continue to run in endless circles, the Self remains untouched.

This Self is indivisible; listener and teacher are one in it. As Karl says, "I talk only to myself." Thus, he suggestively refers to his discourses as "Self-talks, soliloquies in which the Self speaks." Of course, the Self also listens, since any distinction between Self and other can only be the product of thought.

This is the essence of the Indian *Advaita* philosophy ("*A*" means "not" and "*dvaita*" means "dual"; thus "*advaita*" means "non-dual"). In this view, separation is an illusion that is upheld by the mind. As soon as thought rests, the separation disappears, along with desire and fear. Jean Paul Sartre says, "Hell is others." According to Karl, "As long as you believe that others exist, you live in Hell."

Perhaps, Sartre overstates his case; living with stress is Hell enough for most of us. But if anything obliterates Hell and ends stress, it's dialogues like these, with a teacher who knows that Hell doesn't exist and that separation is non-existent.

The living presence of such a teacher may bring us great help, but his printed presence has its advantages, too. You no longer have to endure the breaks and pauses that occur in every talk. Neither do you suffer the discomfort of hard chairs or a harder floor. You can interrupt this eloquent comedian whenever you choose, and you don't have to pay the entrance fee each time you come back to him!

—Dietmar Bittrich
Germany

Preface

The Fire of Awakening

As a child I saw an absolute division in experiences. One moment I was completely detached and in perfect harmony with the world, while the next moment I was in deep depression, wishing for dissolution and death. I was either filled with heavenly happiness or filled with sadness and death. Naturally, I wanted to dwell only in the pleasant experiences, so the search began to achieve this.

Initially, I was not searching for truth or enlightenment, but unlimited happiness—the end of suffering—and thus began the search to find suitable means and tools to achieve this end. I first tried to find it through sex, but because the fulfillment was fleeting and dependent on a partner, it didn't offer a permanent solution. I next experimented with drugs, which created a temporary state of freedom from suffering. However, when the effect was over, it resulted in even more suffering. I then began to read esoteric books about religion, shamanism, and magic, and for a long period Carlos Castaneda, Don Juan, and the possibility of freedom fascinated me.

Around the end of the 1970s, I became spontaneously aware in a dream that I was dreaming. I then remembered a Don Juan technique of observing one's own hands in a dream. So in the dream I lifted my hands and began to investigate them. Suddenly, something awoke in me that had seemingly been dormant. During this awakening, beginning with my hands, my whole body began to dissolve. I recognized the presence of death, and with this recognition a sudden fear arose. Sensing that an unexplainable force that seemed like an infinite black hole was about to extinguish me, I began to fight for my life. The fight continued even when I woke up.

After a number of hours, when I suddenly accepted my extinction, the former darkness became a radiant light, with me being *it,* a light shining in itself. Everything appeared as it was before this experience, except the perception was absolutely detached from what was perceived; there was a total distance and alienation toward the world. My only thought was "This is not my home," after which the "my"-sense lost itself in "I"-lessness. With this awakening of cosmic consciousness, the process of dissolving the concept "Karl" had begun.

Aware of the falsehood and dreamlike quality of my experiences, I knew it was only a matter of time for my personal history, and with it the history of the universe, to be burned up by this fire of awareness. The movement from individual to cosmic consciousness, from personal to impersonal consciousness, which is referred to as enlightenment, is always unique and can neither be repeated nor imitated. Although there is only absolute Being, each experience is absolutely unique.

For nearly fifteen years, this impersonal consciousness was my home. I was a wandering "nothing," absolutely identified with Nothing. The little "I," the owner of Nothing, had become a big, supra-dimensional nothing. The background considered the foreground an illusion. It was like one illusion viewing another! I vaguely considered "not being" to be an advantage over being, and consequently I had a subliminal fear of losing this advantage of clarity.

Only later (from now to now) did absolute cognition come as a simple insight, a little "aha," the realization of being that which is. Being can never be anything else, which means that there's never anything other than the Self, which is prior to all ideas of existence or non-existence.

Toward the end of the 1980s, I suffered from headaches once or twice each week. After approximately one year, the headaches had become daily migraines that I woke up and went to bed with. All attempts to fight them only made them worse. No medicines, whether natural or chemical, could affect them in any way.

I could escape only through sleep or through a kind of meditation. Although I was against any kind of so-called "spiritual practice," this permanent pain had me sink into a condition of absence each morning right after waking up. In this condition, I experienced the pain only as a vibrating light in awareness. In this state no one had the pain. Generally, after four or five hours, I would spontaneously emerge from the meditation, and with the appearance of "me," the pain also appeared. It was like going from heaven to hell. Somehow, throughout it all, I managed to go into the studio and paint, more or less successfully. In this way I created for myself an approximate daily routine.

About four years passed in this manner, until one morning I emerged from meditation after about two hours and turned on the television to watch the stock exchange news. Coincidentally, BBC television was playing the *Mahabharata*, an Indian Gods-and-Heroes-epic in which Lord Krishna conveys to Arjuna (the hero) the lesson that he does not have free will. Despite his pacifist attitude, he has no choice but to engage in battles and wars and kill innumerable opponents— all according to his destiny.

Initially, I immediately wanted to switch back to the stock exchange news, since during this time my career as an artist had plummeted toward zero because of the regular migraines. I was living off the investments I had made, yet, despite financial necessity, something prevented me from switching the channel.

I first watched with little interest, but gradually I began to follow the play's progress. By the end of the epic, most of the characters had died, and Krishna took Yuddhistra, the brother of Arjuna (who was a true disciple), to heaven, where all of his enemies spent their time joyfully. He asked Krishna where his own friends and family were. Krishna answered that they all had landed in hell. "I want to be with them; the relative joy of heaven means nothing to me anymore," said Yuddhistra. So they both took off to hell, where they saw all of his friends and family burning in hellfire and suffering.

Yuddhistra sank into a deep despair. After a while, Krishna asked him whether he could remain in that condition forever.

By this time I was so deeply involved in the play and so completely identified with Yuddhistra that I felt the question was actually addressed to me. He, or I, answered, "I have no desire to change anything or to avoid pain or suffering. If I must remain in this condition for the remainder of my existence, so be it." Meanwhile, my headache increased to such an extent that at this moment an explosion-like experience tore through the back of my head, filling my perception with pure light. At this moment, there was an absolute acceptance of being. Time stopped, Karl and the world disappeared, and a kind of pure *Is-ness* in a glaring light appeared. It was a pulsating silence, an absolute aliveness that was perfect in itself—and I was that.

After what felt like an eternity (about three to four hours of clock time), Karl and the world reappeared, but now the headache was gone. At the same time, I had the absolute acceptance and unconditional knowledge that time only appears in me and what I am is *prior* to time. I saw that everything exists in time and that nothing, not even the slightest sensation, can touch that which is absolute and which is life itself.

Through this series of events and circumstances, which were neither willed, intended, or influenced by "Karl"—*despite* and not *because* of all searching—absolute acceptance, perfect love, the primordial ground of existence became aware of itself.

I didn't have a personal teacher. The Self is the only Master I know. It realizes itself in losing and in finding. In this sense, as both the teacher and disciple, it always gives itself absolute lessons.

The Merry-Go-Round

You can lean back and enjoy your Self
because it always drives directly to happiness.

Welcome! Welcome to the fair! I can see that you're already sitting on the merry-go-round with all its colorful conveyances! It's great how you're driving. You have a sleek car with an accelerator and a brake. Most of all, you have a steering wheel that you can spin around, and that's just what you're doing. Strangely though, as much as you steer it, put your foot down on the throttle, or jam on the brakes, the car keeps traveling in the same direction.

That's how your "I" (the so-called "ego") works. It steers to the left, steers to the right, but is never fully content with the result. It thinks, "I'll take a look at the others. How are they driving? How is that guy doing over there? That one is definitely shifting his weight more in the curve. I think I'll try that, too." But nothing changes. The car keeps on going round and round.

Every now and then the merry-go-round stops, and there's a short break. The Tibetans call this interval between rides the *bardo*, after which you look for another vehicle. You might say, for example, "Let's try the horse this time. I'll ride it for a while. Maybe that's my destiny!" What a very smart choice on your part! Or perhaps to be truly wise, you sit yourself in the big swan car because all this driving has tired you out and left you full of humility.

Doing all this steering, your ego ripens tremendously. And if by chance you were aiming in the same direction as the merry-go-round, you can say triumphantly, "Wow, I did that really well! I think I've got it!" Now you've discovered how all this works. "I have complete control," you say proudly. You're in harmony with the cosmos and with creation. An ego that's so coherent steers in the same direction the merry-go-round is moving. "Look how I can steer," you say happily. "The entire merry-go-round moves because I'm steering this way! Here, look at me!"

If you've mastered the art in this incomparable way, you can even tell others how they should drive. "This is the way you have to do it, like me!" you proclaim.

Now you're a fully awakened driver. "Follow him!" exclaim a few others enthusiastically. Soon you think, "The best thing would be if I just take over the entire bus, so you announce, "Get on board here, everyone, and sit behind me! I'm one with the merry-go-round!" Now you're a guru.

If you want to be active in a quieter way, you can, of course, take on other important jobs, such as driving the fire engine or the ambulance. Or, to be on the safe side, you may just follow the ambulance!

In all this, it's important that you keep the overview. You

must press the gas pedal at the right moment, break at the right moment, and, most of all, steer with great skill because that helps others. In this way, you not only keep your vehicle perfectly on the path, but you also contribute to the successful ride of the entire merry-go-round. If only everyone would drive like this!

You have everything under control until one day you accidentally let go of the steering wheel. Oops! Now you're surprised. It also works on its own! The merry-go-round drives by itself! In just the same way, the Self is driving your life, so you don't have to strain. You can lean back and enjoy your Self because it always drives directly to happiness.

Why Are We here? What Are You Doing, Sitting in a Special Place?

What's real experiences no coming or going. It's not subject to time, and you don't have to do anything to realize it.

Question: What decides that you should sit there in front while I'm here at the back?
Karl: That which placed you there placed me here. But I don't know what it is. It's not a doer, and it has no direction. It has no will and manifests as different aspects of itself—one here, one there.

Q: Then we could switch places, couldn't we?
K: Of course. That, too, would be part of the production. Consciousness plays all the roles: world, space, and time. Consciousness plays every character sitting here. He who talks here also listens there. Because it's all one consciousness, there's no separation.

Q: It's all the same consciousness?

K: It's exactly the same. There's nothing separate.

Q: But consciousness plays the one in front as an enlightened being.

K: There's no enlightened one here or anywhere else. In truth, consciousness plays the speaker as a cup, and such an object can never become enlightened. The cup exists as a form, an appearance. In the same way, the "I" is a form. I am just like a cup and as helpless in attaining enlightenment as anyone else sitting here. We're all absolutely helpless.

Q: Then we're in for a funny evening. Does nothing get clarified here?

K: Nothing. So you don't need to make an effort. There's nothing for you to take away and nothing to carry. If you notice yourself making an effort, it means you want to take something away for yourself. You want to clarify something unnecessarily, like an overactive sewage plant that tries to purify what's already clean.

Q: Is it prohibited to expect some help for our daily life?

K: Not at all. And do you know what can give you the greatest help? Just realize that there's no daily life, only the eternal Now, which is what you are. Nothing comes; nothing goes.

Q: I can't do anything with this.

K: You don't have to. And you can't, anyway, because everything is done to you, through you, and with you. You are the source and that which springs from it. What, then, is daily life? Everything is the eternal Now of your absolute existence.

Q: Everything is absolutely, totally nothing and Now. But aren't there small realizations that allow one to breathe?

K: What gives itself room to breathe will be restricted again. What gets help becomes helpless again. What can wake up falls asleep again. You would need to nurse it constantly— because it's not real. What's real experiences no coming or going. It's not subject to time, and you don't have to do anything to realize it. Be that which is prior to what is or is not. Be that which you cannot not be!

Q: I'll do that. That was a wonderfully helpful description!

K: It wasn't a description. And, moreover, you can't do anything.

Q: That's what I meant to say.

K: It's a pointer towards something that can't be described. It describes itself in everything and nothing. No matter where I'm pointing, I'm always pointing at myself, always towards that which is. Wherever I point, I can never miss myself. There's no direction where the Self isn't.

Q: Am I the Self, too?

K: Yes. That's why you can sit up front now.

What's Going on Here?

The feeling of being completely in love and
completely defenseless is your natural state.

Question: Something is happening here. Something is communicating itself with and without words. It's contagious and remains present.

Karl: For a while the protective shield that filters your ideas is absent, leaving a state of unknowing, a nakedness of any definition. And this remains, realizing itself. In it no idea can hang around. It vibrates within the words, deleting all your ideas, at least until they return. After some time you may recognize that ideas are just ideas.

Q: And is this recognition useful for something?
K: No, not if there remains someone who recognizes it.

Q: True. The one who recognizes is "me." After all, it's the me who wants something to be useful.

K: Nothing can be done about this. The one who recognizes only falls down the manhole when it happens. This is called "grace." The one who recognizes tumbles with a tiny "aha," realizing that nothing ever happened to what really is.

Q: Nothing ever happened, but doesn't nakedness also mean vulnerability?
K: Yes, because there's no more protective shield. Self-realization means being totally defenseless. You empathize with whatever appears in your perception. You can no longer say no to anything. You're entirely that which you perceive and that which exists in your perception. There's no separation between perceiver and perceived.

Q: This sounds overwhelming.
K: Many who experience this and who don't understand it end up in mental hospitals. The filter called "I" doesn't exist anymore. All information from the outside world streams in unfiltered. We discuss it here just in case it occurs so that nobody goes crazy.

Q: Or at least we know why we're going crazy.
K: I can only point out how stupid it is to ward it off. Within the protective shield of the "I"-thought, there's the idea that something exists other than "I"—that there's someone to whom things could happen. But you are that which is without a second, and everything that touches you, everything that you experience, is only yourself. This is Self-realization.

Q: And only our protective shield prevents it?
K: Yes, and I can't remove it from you. If I could, it would

mean something were wrong with you. But there's nothing wrong with having a protective shield as long as it exists. At some point, it will drop—at death, at the very latest. It also could drop right now. Then you would see how you can't defend yourself.

Q: Sometimes I can see that.
K: For example, you can't decide whether or not to fall in love; it simply happens. You're defenseless in this regard. The feeling of being completely in love and completely defenseless is your natural state.

Q: But I clearly can experience that state.
K: And if it's meant to be, you'll no longer experience this relatively, but absolutely.

This means there will be nobody who experiences this state. Nobody could bear it. This empathy, in which everything streams into your awareness and into your emotional world, is unbearable for an "I." But for the Self, it's completely natural.

Q: It sounds strenuous.
K: When grace appears, an emptiness comes into being in which the person no longer exists. With this awareness, the Hell fire appears in which the small "I" can't exist.

Q: Did you say "Hell fire"?
K: Yes. You can call it grace or Hell fire. Nobody can prevent it, and nobody can accelerate it. Grace is a mystery and works in a mystic sphere; it's unconditional and uncontrollable.

Q: But doesn't the presence at satsang bring it about?

K: It may or may not. Presence isn't a condition. Likewise, satsang isn't a condition. There is no condition. Essentially, the possibility always exists.

Q: I've noticed that since I've been coming to satsang more frequently, I have insomnia.

K: Some feel I'm a sleeping pill! If it's destined that the experience of insomnia enables you to realize who you are, then it will happen that way. That which you are is never awake and never asleep. Sleeping and waking appear as states within it, but that which you are doesn't know sleep. This awareness is always completely present, even in deep sleep. If insomnia is your path to this sleepless awareness, how wonderful!

Q: But I get headaches.

K: Why should you fare any better than I? I experienced five years of migraines and insomnia. I was always diving into a cacophony of light and would rarely unwind. Once the energy is released, these phenomena can happen.

Q: It sounds quite tempting.

K: Sleeplessness, electric everywhere, the head an immensely booming bell, with thunderstorms of pain: It was a circus show! Consciousness, which is pure energy, awakens in every cell, in the head, in the entire body. I call it Hellfire because the body panics as the world of thoughts is blown apart. Everything has to go. When absolute intelligence awakens within you, the energy can't slumber. Many call this process enlightenment because of the phenomenon of light in which matter and antimatter fuse and become awareness. There are nuclear reactions like sunspots. Truly, you become a nuclear reactor!

Q: In the past I was against nuclear power.
K: And now perhaps you'll remain quiet because you know the meaning of these symptoms, which are merely accompanying effects. Quietness and silence are always there, with stillness as the source.

Q: Then I might as well simply remain still.
K: As you become more still, the phenomena grow more powerful.

Q: Then there's no escape.
K: Not from your own reactor.

Q: You said it has no protective shield?
K: If it comes to that, it no longer has an operator, either.

I'd Like to Become Enlightened

That which you are doesn't need any
enlightenment. It's never been in the dark.

Question: It may sound old-fashioned, but I want to become enlightened.
Karl: I can only wish you good luck.

Q: What do you mean? Is this desire nonsense?
K: It's not nonsense, but just a bit of mental trickery.

Q: I believe it's slightly more than that.
K: Enlightenment and unenlightenment are ideas. Enlightenment is merely one more concept in that endless stream of ideas about improving yourself, discovering yourself, or obtaining happiness.

Q: And what's wrong with that?

K: It's unnecessary because there's never been any need for anyone to become enlightened.

Q: I doubt that.
K: Who wants to become enlightened?

Q: As I said, "I."
K: So the "I" wants to radiate light.

Q: Of course. Is that prohibited?
K: When it comes to electrical safety regulations, certainly!

Q: What?
K: It's extremely doubtful whether an "I" can stand such energy. In this absolute energy of being, which becomes indescribable light—the "I" burns out. If you shoot ten thousand volts through a light bulb, it bursts, and anything that remains is vaporized.

Q: It has an orgasm.
K: Which, however, it doesn't notice.

Q: Does that mean that I'm a weak bulb?
K: What do you mean by "I"?

Q: I mean that which I am, the "me" that sits in front of you.
K: That which you are doesn't need any enlightenment. It's never been in the dark.

Q: All right, let's forget about the term "enlightenment." Let's call it "awakening."

K: It doesn't need awakening, either, because that which you are has never been asleep.

It knows neither sleeping nor waking. Waking and sleeping appear within it. Moreover, there's no one awake or asleep. There's no enlightened one or someone who needs enlightenment. These meaningless ideas merely appear and disappear in that which you are.

Q: But in order to see or grasp this, wouldn't I need to experience some kind of awakening?

K: The "I" doesn't need awakening. At the moment that you are what you are, there's no more room for the light bulb. It's burned out, vaporized; it disappears as if it never existed. And this is the joke: Indeed, it never has existed. Because wherever that is which is, there's nothing else but that which is.

Q: The where ... the that ... the what! Well, where am I?

K: You're burned out, vaporized; you've disappeared. At least, it seems that way. In truth, though, you didn't exist before, and you won't exist afterward.

Q: So the "I" has to disappear?

K: How can something disappear that was never there?

Q: But I do exist. I'm sitting here. The question is: How much longer? (A cell phone is ringing.)

K: Just answer it. Your electrician wants to know whether he can switch on the current.

Nobody Gets Enlightened

Drop this program of enlightenment or awakening.

Question: Once someone is enlightened, can he ever lose that state?
Karl: Again and again.

Q: Isn't he in it once and for all?
K: No. As long as there's one who's enlightened, that one will emerge again.

There has to be an "aha" in which the Self, which is existence itself, remains forever realized. No person is needed to realize this. Existence doesn't need some kind of phenomenon to realize what existence is.

Q: No, existence doesn't need it, but I do.
K: You don't need it. You can never exist as an enlightened one. And you never existed as an unenlightened one, either.

Drop this program of enlightenment or awakening.

Q: Isn't it necessary to be touched by it at least once?
K: Who or what could be touched? What change would be needed for it to happen? Whatever touches you will disappear again. Every experience of touching is fleeting.

Q: But as a teacher, can't you . . .
K: I'm completely helpless. I am helplessness itself. I can't turn you into something you already are.

Q: Then help me be what I am.
K: Whatever I could try to do would only consolidate your idea that you are not yet that.

Q: Can't you give it a go, anyway?
K: But no one is there who could be improved.

Q: I gladly believe that nobody could improve you. But me . . .
K: You can't be improved, either.

My "I" Wants to Disappear

The illusion of an "I," which again and again
appears in a question, remains irrepressible.

Question: Why was I born?
Karl: Why not? Existence completely agrees with the fact that you are and the way you are. It's perfect. No meaning is necessary. The quest for meaning arises only with the idea of an "I"

Q: All right, but still I ask this question.
K: The "I" is a concept that desires relevance. It poses a question that wants to be satisfied and dissolved by an answer. But then immediately the next question arises. Actually, it's always the same question: "Why am I?" This is the dilemma of the "I." To justify its existence, it has to find a reason to be alive. It tries desperately to prove that it exists but can't find the evidence. That's why it always has a new question, and that's why no answer will ever be enough. Thus, it doesn't

matter whether the question is answered or not. There's only one answer to the question "Why?" That's "Why not?"

Q: Doesn't the "I" have any value at all?
K: Whether valuable or valueless, it proves its existence by seeing itself as worthless: "Poor little me, inadequate me!" Essentially, it desires proof of its own existence. If inferiority is useful as a proof, then it's gladly inferior, poor, and pathetic. The "I" knows all the tricks in the world to survive. It's like a wobbly man. You can knock it over a thousand times, but it always comes up again. Even if it could remain lying down, it would at least exist. The illusion of an "I," which again and again appears in a question, remains irrepressible.

Q: Life must be beautiful when this question is finished once and for all!
K: You mean existence needs to be unquestioning in order to be happier? Perhaps it's as happy asking questions as not asking. "If this or that weren't there . . . If I had got rid of this or that"—All these are merely "I"-ideas. Existence can't be disturbed. It doesn't need to get rid of anything. But the "I"-idea at some point experiences itself as disturbing and then attempts to eliminate all disturbances, including itself.

Q: Yes, that's how I feel.
K: The "I" makes you believe that it has to disappear.

Q: Exactly!
K: But if you believe this, it can continue to exist even longer, undisturbed.

Who Is It That's Spinning this Yarn?

In the awakening of the "I," your
spinning began.

Question: I'm here because I don't want to be reborn.
Karl: And precisely because of this desire it will happen.

Q: What?
K: The desire to avoid something always commands it to happen.

Q: Then tell me how to get rid of this desire.
K: You can't get rid of anything.

Q: How can I get out of my predicament?
K: You can't get out of it. But you can devote yourself to not getting rid of anything, including your predicament! This is Self-realization, the understanding that you can't escape what you are. Lean back and enjoy it. No one else can do it for you.

Q: If I could enjoy life, I wouldn't be here.

K: You're here because you have no choice. You can't do otherwise. You are the freedom that has no choice how it expresses itself. If it had a choice, it wouldn't be freedom. Enjoy this choicelessness, the inevitability of your existence. Real enjoyment is seeing that you can never change what you are.

Q: For me this is pretty much the opposite of enjoyment.

K: I can only tell you that which you are enjoys every moment and the opposite of every moment. It enjoys itself completely. And that which thinks it's not enjoying itself is also part of the enjoyment.

Q: That doesn't get me anywhere, knowing that I'm part of some kind of enjoyment. I want to be the one who enjoys.

K: That which you really are enjoys the non-enjoyment, too!

Q: That's like spinning a yarn.

K: You're right. It's spinning a yarn.

Q: Thank you.

K: But the one who spins it, the spider, is you. You're weaving this endless network of cosmic thoughts and forms. The moment will come when you think, "What's the point of all this spinning? And who does the spinning, anyway? I think I'm spinning! That's it!"

In the awakening of the "I," your spinning began. You're the source of this endless web of war and peace, the entire web of creation. You spin every thought and every form. But in the sudden realization that it's you, the entire web is sucked back. Once you see this, there's neither world nor spinning.

Q: Do you expect me to follow you?

K: Not at all. I'm not sitting here to help you understand something. I'm sitting here so that he who thinks he could understand disappears into non-understanding.

Q: Before I disappear, I'd like to get a couple of solutions.

K: I don't dissolve anything. On the contrary, I create knots.

Q: Yes, I've noticed that.

K: I'm not here to dissolve but to create knots. I tie so many knots in your brain that you may suddenly realize it's impossible to ever undo them. Then you can give up trying and simply be still. Once you're completely still, who cares whether there were ever worlds, rebirths, webs, knots, or dissolutions?

Why Do You Talk So Much?

There's only silence here.

Question: With all the satsang teachers I've known, there are periods of silence, yet you talk constantly.
Karl: There's only silence here.

Q: It's quite a talkative silence!
K: It's a silence that talks and listens.

Q: It's a silence that doesn't like to shut up.
K: The silence doesn't care what comes out of it. It doesn't have any intention. It doesn't differentiate between right and wrong. Neither does that which listens.

Q: You mean to say that the content of what's said makes no difference?
K: The only thing I know is that silence both talks and listens.

Q: That's all?

K: Nothing more.

Q: Does that mean that actually nothing happens here?

K: Yes. And still something always remains.

Q: And that . . .

K: Is silence.

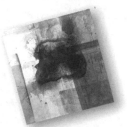

Don't Trust Any Masters, Dead or Alive

All teachings that state that there's a way out of misery keep it going.

Question: You have something that we don't have. At least I feel it. You also sit in front while we sit here. What's your view on this? Are we stupid?

Karl: If I regarded myself as wise and enlightened, only stupid, unenlightened beings would sit in front of me. That would create separation. It would perpetuate the illusion that there's someone here who knows something and someone there who doesn't.

But I talk about knowledge that's absolute: It's absolute here and equally absolute there. This knowledge is nothing new for you. That's why it's nothing you can attain. There's nothing you can discover and nowhere you can arrive. It's already completely present. I talk about that which was never concealed and which doesn't require attainment. Any endeavor can lead only to relative knowledge.

Q: But doesn't every teacher have something to learn?
K: Yes, as long as there's a teacher, he has something to learn.

Q: So there! You *are* a teacher!
K: That's impossible. I can't teach you anything!

Q: But that's what I'm here for.
K: I can't teach you what you are. I can't give you anything. At the same time, I can't remove anything from you, either. If anyone tells you he can give you something, remove anything, or give you enlightenment experiences, that person is a liar.

Q: Then Buddha is a liar.
K: Yes. Don't trust a dead master.

Q: Well, it's not that easy. Buddha has a teaching that life is suffering, and all suffering comes from desire. To escape this, he taught the Eightfold Path.
K: In the *Diamond Sutra*, he said, "No Buddha has ever entered the world, and there never will be one, either." He also said, "For forty years I preached, and I never said a thing. Nobody said anything. Nobody talked and nobody listened."

Q: But the Eightfold Path exists as a Dharma teaching.
K: There are people who carry one teaching by repeating the same old words. These parrots, who maintain the traditional concepts, keep the misery alive. All teachings that state that there's a way out of misery keep it going. They keep the conceptual process going so long that they become constipated.

Q: Let's take as another example, the entire *Bhagavad Gita*, which consists of a teaching dialogue between Krishna and Arjuna.

K: Krishna, Buddha, Jesus, and Socrates are all appearances. They appear to show you a way out of your dilemma. Each one of them appears to show you a picture with a beautiful goal, or at least a hole in the wall where you can get through.

You only have to make the effort to jump high enough, and you can achieve the goal. You only have to squeeze tightly enough, and then you can get through the hole in the wall.

In the end, you only have to muster enough courage to take the final step into the abyss.

Q: And all this isn't true?

K: You just can't jump high enough. Nobody can take the last step into the abyss of existence inside you. Only the Self can take it, and the Self doesn't need to take this step because it's the abyss! The Self is the total abyss, the absolute nothingness.

Q: Do you mean to say that you can't help me?

K: That's right.

Q: That's impossible.

K: In the relative, everything is possible; in reality, nothing is.

Q: It doesn't matter. I still like to sit here.

K: Remember what I said earlier: Nobody sits here who says something, and nobody sits over there who hears it. Because the hearer and the speaker are one, there's no separation.

Whether the speaking comes out of this body or the hearing happens in that body, it doesn't matter. That which speaks here and listens there is one.

Q: I don't experience that at all, yet I feel that what you say is helpful. It reminds me of something.
K: Perhaps it reminds you of yourself.

Q: Yes, perhaps that's what it's about.
K: I don't give you anything; I just throw you back on yourself. I throw everything back at you. You give it to me; I give it to you; I give me to me.

Q: You to you?
K: We play hide-and-seek with ourselves.

Q: And that's what I meditated for all these years!
K: Exactly. Everything that did and didn't happen prepared you for this, so it can happen in this way. There's nothing wrong with this. It's always right; it always happens at the right moment—now.

Q: Therefore, I shouldn't trust dead masters.
K: That's right. Don't trust dead masters. There aren't any living ones, either.

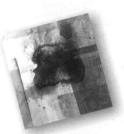

What Can a Teacher Do?

*The master/disciple relationship is fiction
because in truth only the source exists.*

Question: What makes a teacher into a teacher and a disciple into a disciple?

Karl: Eventually, someone thinks he needs to learn something, and someone else thinks he's got something to teach. A disciple believes he needs more knowledge to get closer to his goal. A teacher thinks he has something to teach the disciple. In relative life, it's true. If you want to learn to drive a car, you need a driving instructor. One has the information, and the other can learn.

Q: And isn't that the case in the spiritual sphere? Because the teacher sees that everything is one while the disciple doesn't, the teacher can help. In many traditions, this relationship has existed for thousands of years.

K: Yes, the guru/disciple relationship has a long history, and if it's supposed to be that way, it's the right thing. However, what we talk about here happens not because of but in spite of master/disciple relationships. The Self simply becomes aware of itself. The concept of master and disciple is irrelevant.

Q: The tradition clearly states that without a master, it's impossible to be realized. It only works through a master.
K: It only works through the Self. The Self may reveal itself in the form of a master, but it could also be a book or something else.

Q: The tradition states that the master has to be alive, which means in a body. Only in this living form can he help a disciple unravel the entanglement of his mind.
K: A living master can help the disciple reach cosmic consciousness, using many possibilities of guidance. For example, the disciple may use either the approach of *neti, neti* ("not this, not this") or "You are not the body." Both hint at what you are not. All questions like "Who am I?" help the individual consciousness become cosmic.

Q: Do you deny that such methods work?
K: Nothing ever happens through something else, but always through the source. Therefore, it's always spontaneous, natural, and never conditional. The master/disciple relationship is fiction because in truth only the source exists. Everything emerges from it, and everything returns to it. Within this dream there are master/disciple meetings, but they don't affect anything. All effects come only from the source.

Q: But the source works through the master. It works through him more than anyone else.

K: No, the source works in all equally and uniquely. It needs nothing special. Whatever happens, including the awakening to cosmic consciousness, happens for no reason, but simply because it happens.

Q: What about devotion and the emphasis on surrender, which play an important role in the tradition?

K: What belongs to you that you can give up? To whom should it be given? You have the illusion of being a person who can own something and whose ownership can be given up. Who needs this to happen? To whom can it occur?

No matter how one gets from individual to cosmic consciousness, what's involved is merely a change of states. You get from A to B, but who takes this step and who gains an advantage from it? Is there anyone whose individual consciousness is disadvantaged? If there were, it would mean that the Self could only be natural in cosmic consciousness, while in individual consciousness there'd be something wrong or provisional. But both are the same consciousness.

Death also ends the individual consciousness, transforming it into formlessness, but it becomes form again at the first opportunity. Both are the same consciousness. One is in time, while the other is in no-time, that's all. The absolute isn't conditioned by any state.

Q: How do you know this?

K: Nobody can know it. Whatever I say is a concept. The only thing you can't doubt is that "I" am prior to all concepts. I only know that I am not a concept; I exist and that's all I really know. I first have to exist even to talk about a concept. Existence is the only thing beyond any doubt, while every concept about it remains open to question.

Q: In that case, why are we sitting here?
K: You're recognizing that everything is a concept arising from your idea of an "I," and it can't touch what you are. You can let everything appear and disappear, yet something always remains that's beyond words, existing before, after, and in-between all concepts. This is the primordial ground of existence, which can't be learned or realized because it's you. For this you don't need to do anything. You don't have to make an effort; you don't have to drop anything, nor do you not have to let go. Any idea you have, any attempt to do or refrain from doing something to achieve it, can't make you into what you already are.

Q: I have visited many masters, for whom the master/disciple relationship was most important. Did I fall prey to a concept?
K: The concept disappears; everything disappears, including every differentiation, every idea of value or quality. What remains is the only thing that exists. In the absence of all concepts, peace appears in it. This includes the absence of any idea about master/disciple relationships. Such an idea is as fictitious as the belief that you live. The idea of a master appears only where there is the idea of an "I."

If you truly had respect for your masters, you would simply let them disappear. You would recognize your master as what you are. At such a moment, there would be no more masters and disciples. With such respect for what is, you would bring happiness to all the masters of this world.

No master ever said, "Raise me to the heavens and build me a church. They all said, "Forget me as soon as I'm gone. If you want to honor me, forget me." But followers didn't listen to their words, but instead founded new religions. Jesus never said, "Found a religion." He said, "Let the dead bury the dead."

Q: You want to run down the masters for me!

K: What you're really doing is avoiding the emptiness, for which there are many techniques. The master/disciple relationship is your attempt to fill the emptiness by creating an object, a goal for your "I" to attain. The whole thing is completely irrelevant. The "I" is simply an idea of separation that needs an object and thus a goal. Any goal is good enough, even the goal to abolish all goals!

This approach, too, can fill the space of your emptiness. The "I" is tricky, and you can't escape it. It even hides behind the not-hiding. The doer hides behind the non-doer.

Q: So what can I do?

K: Do only what you can't do. What is always completely itself under all circumstances? What is it that never experiences any change in itself? What is the most solid thing there is? What is this primordial ground, which always has to be there in order for a realizer and a realization to exist at all? What is this essence, which is always still, which never moves, within which information simply appears and disappears?

Tell me. For you to become that which is permanent, which neither comes nor goes, what has to happen? Do you have to do something? Do you have to realize something, or is it just there, with or without any realization?

Q: I'm sure you're right, but if you meet another teacher who has seen this, don't you have anything to tell each other?

K: The same thing will happen as now because I'm talking to him right now. From your perspective, it may seem that someone sits here who speaks, and someone else sits there who listens. But it's one and the same Self. In this moment he experiences himself as the experiencer, the experiencing, and that which is experienced.

Any idea of separation is fiction. And all other fictions come from the belief that this fiction is real. The question of meaning belongs to this, too. The source, existence, has no need for meaning.

Q: This is the burial of the teacher!

K: The more you recognize this as the only reality, the more will be buried. Whatever you are not will be buried. More and more falls into the eternal grave of irrelevance. More and more beliefs drop until you realize that anything you believe—or feel you ought to believe—can't be the Self.

Q: But the teacher helps me realize that!

K: You believe he has the carrot that you've chased all your life, and when you're mature, he'll serve it to you. Once you've eaten it, you can relax, for then you'll be enlightened. All this is fiction. The awakening from individual to cosmic consciousness is fiction. If you think, "Yes, now I've attained reality and I am all this," it's pure fiction.

Q: But what if this awakening is connected to an existential shock?

K: Everything is part of the dream, including the one who's shocked, too. That which you are is unchanged and untouched by all this. It's what it always was.

Q: Do I have to experience this before the shock will go?
K: Then there will be nobody there to be shocked.

Q: And is that good?
K: It's neither good nor bad, but simply as it's always been. This is nothing new. And if someone asks you, "How's it going?" you'll simply say, "As usual." At that point the teacher taps you on the shoulder and gives you an "A."

Emptiness Teaches

Emptiness is the master of "I." It doesn't do anything; it's simply empty.

Question: I've heard it said that emptiness is the true teacher. Is it so?

Karl: The true teacher always sits between the chairs where it's most comfortable. He doesn't sit here on this chair or there on the next one either, but in the gap between them. The true teacher sits between the moments and between two thoughts. That gap is awareness.

Q: In that case, should I listen to what's between your words?
K: If you're able to. It's hard for the mind because it doesn't like gaps. Your mind can't exist inside the gap.

Inside it there's no mind. Therefore it's said, "Attention, Mind, mind the gap!" Inside it you don't, you won't exist anymore. You can't exist there!

Emptiness is the master that blows away the mind. In

emptiness the mind evaporates. When you're in the gap, you fit perfectly. Since there are no prescribed dimensions, you're the greatest and the smallest, everything that's possible and impossible, infinite space and no space at all—in short, all of existence.

Q: I once took a course in drumming in which I always had to endure the interval, the gap. I could hardly stand it. My feet always wanted to skip over it.

K: Nobody can bear the gap. Emptiness is the master of "I." It doesn't do anything; it's simply empty. There's no "I," yet what you are is completely present.

Even in emptiness this presence is totally there, just as it is here and now. It's never gone; it never comes or goes. It's here, now and always, in the eternal Now. In time there are only hints of that which has no time, only hints of that which has no coming or going, no birth or death. The Self never appears or disappears, yet everything that appears within the Self disappears because it was never there.

Q: At least it fills the gap. Perhaps that's why the gap is so heavy that one can hardly bear it.

K: The emptiness is so light that it's unbearable. Therefore, you fight and kick to fill it.

Q: What if I stopped all this kicking?

K: Forget it. I'll show you how wonderful it is inside the gap, how light! Only your resistance is heavy. It becomes heavy if you try to fill the emptiness. Emptiness itself is completely light, and it's here where you belong.

Q: It's where I'm at home.

K: It's where no home exists.

Q: Is that supposed to be fulfillment?

K: No. These are empty promises.

Q: Oh, I can't grasp you! You dodge every statement like a snake!

K: But the snake says, "Why don't you try it? Come into the gap where you can't exist. Take a bite of the apple!"

Q: And then there's a worm inside.

K: Yes, and you're off into the worm hole, like in *Star Trek*! When you enter the worm hole, you travel in a different dimension. The gap is the drive that pulls you in totally.

Q: Please, no . . . (the bell rings)

K: You're in luck this time.

The Teacher Is Irrelevant

Disciple and teacher disappear, and what remains is life, which is reality itself, absolute existence.

Question: Can a teacher bring a disciple into unity consciousness?

Karl: It's irrelevant. Wherever you can go, you must leave again. The idea of duality may depart for a time, and unity may shine forth, but out of this oneness, duality always emerges again.

Q: But through practice or a teacher, one can have this experience.

K: But wherever effort, techniques, or teachers may bring you, you'll emerge again.

Q: My spiritual teacher said, "You can already experience the unity that comes to everyone after death."

K: Perhaps he means that what follows death has always

been what you experienced in life. The unity always appears again in your awareness. In death the body disintegrates, and body consciousness changes into unity consciousness. But it's still consciousness, and whatever happens in consciousness can't make you into what you are. Experiences of oneness or greater awareness are only experiences, after all. At best, they show you that you're that which experiences, and that which experiences can never be experienced.

Because all experiences, including life and death, are fleeting, they come and go. What you are doesn't come and go. You're the source, and all the phenomena of life are just reflections.

Q: I believe I experienced this once.
K: It can't be experienced. The eye can't see itself. Perception can't perceive itself. Whatever can be perceived isn't what perception is.

Q: But in your case, it also changed, didn't it? Wasn't there a sudden realization?
K: That was simply an "aha." That showed me that what's being perceived can't be what perceives. Even the perceiver is only part of the perceived. What's prior to Little Karl is what really exists, and that can't be experienced. The unfathomable and incomprehensible, total "I"-lessness and desirelessness, are always there, no matter what happens. This is what you are. Whatever appears in front of you is nothing but a reflection of your existence. What you are is the essence of all, which can never be experienced.

Q: Then what's the point? Something that can't be

experienced can't be enjoyed, either.

K: It's a complete dropping away of any desire for phenomena.

Q: Yes, I notice the first signs of that, too. The interest in superficial phenomena decreases. It's a kind of development, perhaps some form of precondition for the "aha."

K: There are no preconditions for it. It's unconditionality itself.

Q: There are no conditions?

K: It's unconditional.

Q: Then I don't need a teacher, either.

K: Who doesn't need a teacher?

Q: What?

K: Who is it that doesn't need a teacher?

Q: Who? What?

K: You can't do anything! Within the dream a teacher and a disciple may appear. Perhaps the disciple thinks he's learned something, but the only thing that happens in this "relationship" is that they both drop away. Disciple and teacher disappear, and what remains is life, which is reality itself, absolute existence.

Q: And what kind of teacher disappears?

K: It can be a personal teacher.

Q: But his only purpose is to disappear?

K: The entirety of life is the teacher.

Q: But doesn't that disappear into the "aha" experience, too?
K: Whatever doesn't exist disappears.

Q: Recently I told a teacher that my entire life is my teacher, and he replied, "No, that's an escape. You need a personal teacher. You need me."
K: A verse in the Vedas says, "As long as there is a teacher who thinks he has something to teach, he still has something to learn."

Q: Yes. When I expressed similar thoughts, this teacher became angry.
K: I hope I remain as irrelevant as always, as irrelevant as I can be!

Q: Does that mean useless?
K: Yes, useless and irrelevant.

Q: Is that your essence, so to speak?
K: Yes, I'm entirely irrelevant.

Q: You're nutty!

Is There Anything I Can Do?

Which Buddha has ever made an effort to become a Buddha?

Question: Bankei, a 17th century Zen master, praised the undivided Buddha mind that's beyond all unity. What is that?
Karl: It's what existed prior to Buddha—"Para-Buddha." What's prior to everything knows neither duality nor unity. It's neither one nor two, neither this nor that. It has no definition, it has all names or none, and it can never comprehend itself.

Q: Perhaps that's why Bankei said, "It's meaningless to strive for it." He told his disciples, "Just stop it!"
K: When you're totally resigned and accept that you'll never be able to comprehend yourself or know yourself, absolute silence comes. When there's no more desire to know yourself, this means you know yourself. Accept that you can never escape and never comprehend your Self because you're that

which is endless, unborn, and immortal. You need nothing within time for this realization, nor do you need any effort. In fact, all effort is futile.

Q: Bankei said, "A much shorter way than effort to become Buddha is simply to be Buddha."
K: Well, then, leave this Bankei.

Q: But Buddha worked hard for many years before he came to his realization. Would he have reached enlightenment without this effort, or did he see it this way afterward?
K: What do you think? Where did the effort come from?

Q: It came from his decision not to change his life.
K: And where did this decision come from?

Q: From his desire to end suffering.
K: And where did this desire come from?

Q: Do you want to continue questioning me like this forever?
K: Wittgenstein asked the question, "If there were a free will, who could have it?"

Q: Well, a Buddha, for example, could have it.
K: Which Buddha has ever made an effort to become a Buddha?

Q: The one who suffers makes an effort to become a Buddha. One who enjoys himself is probably happy to be reborn many times.
K: You mean that as long as the Self enjoys duality, it chooses

to remain in this relative state, and it frees itself only when this condition becomes uncomfortable. As if the Self could ever be disturbed by itself!

Q: I'm talking about a normal human being, not an abstract Self.

K: You're talking about consciousness that appears to be in a state experienced as pleasant or unpleasant.

Q: No, I'm talking about a human being who makes an effort. I just can't believe that every effort is irrelevant. All the mystics have gone a long way. Even the highly esteemed Ramana Maharshi fought for years to discover the nature of the "I am."

K: As far as I know, he realized it on a single afternoon. That's how it's described on a wall in the ashram at Tiruvannamalai. A foreboding of death came over him, he lay down on the floor, he gave himself to this death experience, and he realized.

Q: Maybe, but that was only the beginning of a long path.

K: It was the beginning and the end. After that experience, he said that nothing further happened to him . . .

Q: Except that he retreated into a cave for years to meditate without disturbance.

K: From that moment on, he said, that his Self could never be disturbed by anything. This was the basic experience of everything.

Q: It may have been the basic experience; nevertheless, some kind of refining was still necessary.

K: You mean it was like taking a seminar at the university. First, you prepare, then you experience it, and then you refine it so it has a lasting effect.

Q: Yes, that's not as far off the point as it sounds. With this one experience, Ramana realized that he was not the body. But at that moment he still had not experienced what he truly was.

K: He didn't experience it because it can't be experienced!

Q: Why not?

K: To have an experience, at least two things are necessary: one who experiences and something that's experienced.

Q: So what?

K: What I'm pointing out isn't an experience. It's simply existence as such, which is completely present here and now. You don't need anything special for this, neither preparation nor refining. It's simply realized, and it's nothing special. As Meister Eckhart put it, it's the primordial ground, pure awareness of existence.

Q: But it's something special, as demonstrated by the intensity of the charisma, the infinite kindness, and undisturbed stillness of the masters who attained it. Whoever meditated with Ramana attained *samadhi* (cosmic consciousness).

K: Cosmic consciousness is nothing special. It's simply an experience, but I'm talking about the Self. The stillness you mention has nothing to do with whether one can sit still or be still externally and internally. That stillness is unassailable:

It can't be touched by anything, and it knows no thoughts. It's not an experience; it's the Self.

Q: People who came to Ramana or other mystics experienced this stillness. They tasted it and wanted this taste forever. Therefore, they sat down and meditated. I simply don't believe that it doesn't matter whether one makes an effort or not. You imply that nothing one can do will help or hinder it at all. It will just happen at one time or another.

K: No, it doesn't just happen. This stillness, this basic awareness, isn't conditioned by anything, so it can't be influenced by anything that happens in time. Whether, when, and how it happens is entirely independent of all happenings in the temporal realm. Therefore, any action, endeavor, understanding, or non-understanding is pointless. It has no effect on this one small "aha" that is awareness of the absolute.

Q: But it's apparently very significant for the personal life.

K: You hope for an advantage, but there's none. You hope to escape from yourself, but that's impossible. You want to find a way out, but none exists. That which is here doesn't need a way out and will never find one because that which is here is now and eternal. It's infinite! You can't walk towards it, and you can't walk away from it.

Q: But until you do some work or preparation, you won't be ready for this experience, or "non-experience," as you call it. Even to accept what you're saying, effort is needed. Isn't that right?

K: The acceptance doesn't come from what you believe to be, but from the same source as the non-acceptance. Whether you can accept or not isn't in your hands, though you may have the feeling that it was acquired through your efforts.

Q: Exactly.

K: But I know with absolute certainty that you didn't acquire it through any work. Acceptance is a spontaneous occurrence.

Q: That may be, but perhaps you can help this spontaneity to happen.

K: No effort helps. There's no preparation, and no final polishing is required.

Q: But with other spiritual teachers, I experience that deep sharing is very helpful.

K: That sounds good.

Q: There's a deep exchange of feelings.

K: You mean sheep sharing?

Q: No, there's a deep exchange, a sharing of the depth.

K: To share the depth? To split it with a knife so there are two depths?

Q: No, I don't mean to part, but to participate in each other's feelings; in fact, to share all feelings, even those that hurt.

K: One shears them short.

Q: One is open and honest and doesn't deal with them in a rush.

K: Instead, one deals with them slowly, with a dull knife, so it hurts. Your deep sharing sounds like pulling your hair out slowly! Do I view it correctly?

Q: No, not at all.
K: Sheep shearing is normally done with a sharp knife to make it go faster.

Q: So there's indeed a meaningful preparation—the sharpening of the knife!
K: In the end, when all the hair is gone, you're naked and nothing is left.

Q: And it's all thanks to good preparation.
K: You've defeated me. Are there any other questions that I can't answer?

What Can I Do Myself?

The Self knows one hundred percent what it needs to find itself.

Question: Ramana Maharshi says that there's no such thing as karma and rebirth. Yet I find that with my awareness of the ego, these still exist.

Karl: As long as there's the concept of "I," everything else arises, including ideas of dirt and the need for purification, along with desires to improve the quality of life. Within this framework of concepts, you can talk about everything. But all these concepts appear only when the "I" appears and it's accepted as real.

Q: So there's no preparation whatsoever?

K: For what—a heavenly state, a paradise, a magnificent goal? With the idea that we've lost something or need to reach a goal, we create Hell for ourselves. We then believe that we have the free will to choose, to strive, to make effort. All this comes from the "I"-thought, which produces the belief that we live in separation, which is Hell. The "I" thought and Hell appear simultaneously. This is diabolical. "Dia" means two. *Dia-bolo*, the Devil, is the one who creates two-ness.

Q: There's a Devil?
K: Exactly. The "I" is the Devil. But the "I" doesn't exist, since it's only an idea. How, then, can I abolish this Devil, which doesn't exist? What can I do about it? What can an idea do about an idea, a concept about a concept, and an illusion about an illusion?

Q: Not much, apparently.
K: Do I have to do something about it at all?

Q: Perhaps a little practice would help?
K: I simply have to be what I am.

Q: I was afraid of that.
K: In truth, I am prior to time, the Devil, God, and every idea of existence. I can't "do" anything about this because it's what I am anyhow. What's prior to all doing and experience, movement and nonmovement, time and definition is stillness.

Q: Okay, if nobody exists anymore, then nobody needs to do anything. But somebody exists here!
K: You're sitting here in order to meet yourself and to have that experience.

Q: Yes, in order to have another experience, I meditate.
K: Meditations, efforts, and actions are all wonderful. Ramana

says, "Every step that has ever been taken has led to me and was right."

Q: Good, then I'm not entirely off, then?

K: There are only right steps and right effort. The Self knows one hundred percent what it needs to find itself. At every moment it knows that completely, and it always takes the right step towards itself.

Q: I believe it. But why am I sitting here now?

K: Because the Self has placed you there.

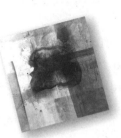

You Can't Do Anything Wrong

Only the Self speaks, and only the Self listens.

Question: Sometimes I feel that now or at any other moment the breakthrough will happen that will finally be it!
Karl: In other words, "I was never as close to me as yesterday evening."

Q: Yes, it's like that.
K: And then you desire to keep this absorption, or closeness, as long as possible. This desire to keep it destroys it again. Essentially, all that remains is the desire.

Q: Yes, and then I'm disillusioned.
K: Disillusionment should be the end of illusion. That's what you're actually looking for—the absolute disillusionment that makes you give up your search entirely. But as long as you're sitting here, you're still deceived.

Q: I'm sitting here to speed things up a little.

K: Whoever thinks it's easier to find himself here than elsewhere is deceived.

Q: Then I don't need to come here! I might as well do whatever I like.

K: You can never do what you like.

Q: My experience is different.

K: Actually, you're being played. You're really helpless and powerless. There's no other being that you could rule over. There's no existence that could have power over another existence.

God's omnipotence is complete impotence. Omnipotence simply means being what you are.

Q: Then I can sit at home and not do anything at all.

K: Well and good! But come back sometime and tell me how it was, and, most of all, whether you succeeded.

Q: To tell the truth, I tried it already and it's difficult.

K: Everybody tries it, and nobody ever succeeds.

Q: Is there nothing one can do?

K: One can only not do anything. You don't do anything; everything happens on its own!

Q: Then I can't do anything wrong, either.

K: Everything you do is exactly right. You can't do anything wrong because you never did or could do anything at all. This is freedom, freedom from the doer, from the person who never did or could do anything!

Q: Who then makes war?
K: You! Who else?

Q: What?
K: You're responsible.

Q: But didn't you just say . . .
K: War and peace exist because you do. You're the source of both. You're responsible for all that exists.

Q: I'm responsible for everything?
K: Yes, because you're all that exists.

Q: Then who are you talking to now?
K: I'm talking to myself.

Q: Thank God!
K: As always. I only talk to that which understands, never to that which doesn't. Isn't that self-evident?

Q: No.
K: Whatever exists is the Self, whether it speaks, listens, or simply stays silent.

Q: Is it just myself, then, that I'm hearing at this moment?
K: You can only listen to yourself. Only the Self speaks, and only the Self listens.

Q: And what's the point of all this?

K: Self-realization.

What Can I Decide?

Nothing depends on you, on this "I" that thinks it's making decisions; actually, every idea is spontaneous.

Question: Can I decide to be aware?

Karl: It's not a decision, but simply an awakening, just like what happens each morning in your bed. You can't decide whether to wake or not. At the moment of awakening, it's decided, spontaneously, naturally, and without thought. You know it well: First, you're in deep sleep, and then bang! you're thrust into awareness. In exactly this way, all of existence comes about. Before it happens, neither the idea nor the desire to wake exists. It simply happens, and from this awakening comes the Big Bang. However, it's nobody's decision; nothing has ever been decided.

Q: Doesn't the "I" decide where and when to direct its attention?

K: This, too, isn't decided. If anything, it's grace. If awareness becomes aware of itself, it's not because of an "I" that decides to pay a bit more attention. You can sit there for a thousand years deciding for awareness to arise, and nothing will happen. Perhaps you've done this already.

Q: I hope so.

K: Or maybe it's ahead of you. In either case, it's not in your hands. Nothing depends on you, on this "I" that thinks it's making decisions. Every idea is spontaneous, every apparent decision comes out of nothing, out of the blue, from the great beyond. It has no direction. In fact, nothing has a direction.

Q: This sounds hopeless.

K: It's neither hopeless, nor does it create hope. Either state would mean that one exists who needs or could have hope. A hopeless or a hopeful one exists as long as you believe in this idea. Only then do these questions come up.

The root is the idea that you exist as an "I." You need to get to the stillness in which all your ideas disappear.

Q: Yes, that's what I want. I've made my decision.

K: Did you ever contribute to anything?

Q: I think so.

K: Simply see that any contribution you made always happened on its own. It operated on its own and didn't need your decision. You fear that, without your decision, nothing would happen, but that's just an idea.

Q: What about the fear that if I make the wrong decision, I will cease to exist?

K: That's the fear of death. It comes when you see that your free will doesn't exist and that you can't control anything. Then the "I" defends itself, thinking that it has something to lose—not just its power to decide, but its very life. Of course, this fear will arise. The separate self's desire to maintain its role in life struggles to survive. The ball keeps rolling, afraid to stop. It's rolling without control, but fears that it might not be a ball anymore if the rolling ended.

Q: Am I still there when the rolling ends?
K: When the role is played to the end, the "I" ends. The "I" is put together from a personal history of doing things. The idea that this history could end awakens fear.

Q: So what happens when personal history stops?
K: It continues just as before, but without your idea of doing something, without any notion of desire, will, control, freedom, or the possibility of making decisions. It continues without any thought of a personal history.

Q: It continues without the person, without me?
K: Yes, just like now. Is there a history now? Look at what's really happening. Just see. Does anything actually change as a result of your decision? Do you make any decision at all? Can you ever grab a desire and change it? Has there ever been anything you could control?

Q: I want to lift my hand. There, you see, I lift my hand.
K: A nerve is stimulated, the hand rises, and immediately the "I" comes rushing in and claims, "I've decided this!" Look carefully at your thoughts, the "I" always comes afterward.

Every action, idea, and thought occurs on its own. But there's a super-idea called "I," which reinterprets every event as part of its own history. A thought by the name of "I" leaps in a moment after an event takes place, claiming the action as its own and calling it "MY will, MY mistake, MY body, MY life, MY death."

Q: Perhaps I begin to understand.
K: YOU understand? Then watch YOUR understanding! See when it occurs, this "YOUR"!

Q: Do you mean that my decision isn't my decision and my desire isn't my desire?
K: Simply be aware. See where the desire comes from. Can you desire to desire? Or does desire emerge from itself as energy unfolding, like a flower that blooms, without reason or meaning? Essentially, desire comes and goes by itself.

Q: At least when it's fulfilled, it goes.
K: It doesn't go through fulfillment. The primordial desire that lies behind all others is the desire for Self-realization, and this desire will never be fulfilled.

Q: So should I forget about this desire, too?
K: There's no hope that you can ever know your-Self. The desire for Self-realization appears only after all other desires have come and gone, without giving you anything. Only then does the desire for Self-realization arise because now you accept the idea that your happiness and peace depend on finding the Self.

Q: Is that wrong?

K: There's simply nothing to find and nothing to realize. The desire for Self-realization appears and has to disappear in the giving up of all searching. When searching ceases, this desire ends.

Q: So I only have to stop searching?

K: Sure, but you can't decide to do it or not. And what's so beautiful is that you don't have to decide. The searching (that is, the desiring) can't disappear through a desire. The last desire can disappear only if desirelessness becomes aware of itself.

Through desire and hard work, you seem to make decisions and control your own progress, and then bang! Through some kind of accident, all this falls away.

Q: And then I'm no more?

K: Yes. It's almost a pity because you had built up such an interesting relationship with yourself.

Welcome to the Ocean of Light

*Real knowledge, as such, doesn't belong to
one who knows or who doesn't know.*

Question: What is possible or achievable for a human
being?
Karl: For a human being, nothing's possible. A human being
is just an idea. And for an idea, nothing's possible. But for
that which you really are—existence itself—there's no
limitation.

Q: That's very well and good for existence, but I'm a little
human being.
K: As long as you define yourself as a human being and live
within the limitations created by this definition, nothing's
possible. Allow yourself to be the "I am," prior to any limits.
Abandon individual consciousness and be cosmic
consciousness, which is pure unity. And then, prior to this
consciousness, be the pure "I." Even this "I" vanishes into

existence, where there's no idea of any "I." This happens at the very end in death. Any idea of being a human being dies, and there's only existence.

Q: Well, then, I can be happy.
K: Be happy now. Existence doesn't lose its perfection, whether it unfolds as "I," "I am," or "I am a human being." In all aspects of this trinity, perfection is still there. Existence is perfect even as a human being. But to limit yourself to this last link of the chain is a crazy idea. You've forgotten that you're the whole. Therefore, you don't have to go back. You've always been the totality of this existence. It's you! You never were the idea "I," "I am," or "I am a human being." You've never been any of these, which are nothing more than ideas.

Q: For thousands of years human beings have been searching for the ultimate realization and haven't found it.
K: The ideas we have about being a separate person and searching for realization form a template through which existence has the experience of human life. However, what eternally experiences itself is always existence. In its experience of being human, it merely reflects itself. As pure existence it can't experience itself, so to have an experience, it needs an experiencer, an "I" and a "you."

Q: Then I'm nothing but a means through which existence has fun.
K: You have this fun your-Self! After all, you're nothing less than the perfect Self-experience in the unfolding of existence. There's only the unfolding of perfection. Every idea of imperfection is nothing but an idea.

Q: But obviously I cling to the idea. Evidently, I don't know any better.

K: "Not knowing" is also a perfect unfolding of knowledge and of what you really are. The one who knows and the one who doesn't know are both appearances. Real knowledge, as such, doesn't belong to one who knows or who doesn't know. A "knower" comes about only with the ideas of time and separation. At that moment you experience separate existence.

Q: Well, then, where is unity?

K: It's here. The separate person you take yourself to be is merely a story you're telling yourself, and you experience what you believe. What is here? "Here" is a light-ocean of vibrations. But from the experiences of your past, you put together a picture drawn from the experiences of objects and people that have continuity in space and time. As a baby you had the experience of light and vibrations in space, not the experience of "chair" and "Mama," which came later.

This moment of space and time exists through your conditioning, your history, your parents, and your environment. They tell you, "That's how it is here, my dear." But it's simply a belief. It appears real because you repeat it to yourself daily.

Q: So I create it from the past, and when it's gone, there's only this moment, now.

K: Then you no longer define everything, saying, "This is a floor, that's a ceiling, this is a chair, and that's death."

Q: Nevertheless, there are differences.

K: They're not there! Experience requires time, but in the now, where are they?

Q: But you see this chair here, don't you?

K: There is seeing.

Q: You see different human beings, don't you?

K: I see differences, but not different human beings.

Q: Wow! You see differences!

K: What's wrong with that? I see differences and realize that they exist only in time, governed by the idea of separation. They depend on existence, which is the only thing essential for this here and now. Everything else is fiction. You are existence, which in this eternal Now looks within itself and thus experiences itself. This is your truth, your Self-realization. This essence realizes itself in all forms, which are fleeting shadows within it.

Q: Yes, I can feel that. Just now I'm trying to . . .

K: I know, you want to make it into an experience.

Q: I'm trying to feel this moment completely. Isn't it possible?

K: Who's asking now? All questions exist in time, while the eternal Now has no questions. So who asks the question— existence or an object in space and time?

Q: Let's put it this way: The question simply came out.

K: That's a good answer. Nothing stands in the way to your enlightenment.

Does Progress Exist?

The ideas that somehow you might avoid suffering by acting one way rather than another creates suffering.

Question: I saw on TV how children were killed by napalm. In the past I couldn't have watched it, but this time I remained surprisingly calm.

Karl: You mean to say that you've made progress? Have you gained something you didn't have before?

Q: I simply wasn't so entangled.

K: A witness consciousness may have emerged, which is no longer involved in a series of events.

Q: Yes, exactly. And I think if something terrible happens to me, I could stay calm in spite of it.

K: Then you're saved?

Q: Well, at least I don't suffer, since I can remain outside of the experience, so to speak.

K: Who remains where? What's the difference whether you remain here or there, whether you're "involved" or "outside"? Who gains something from not being involved? What are you?

Q: I'm the one who's sitting here.

K: And what advantage do you have in your existence? On the contrary, it creates an absolute disadvantage. As long as you exist as a person who wants to gain an advantage from anything, such personal advantage is an absolute disadvantage.

Q: I'm concerned with freedom from suffering.

K: What's truly free doesn't need freedom. The only cause of suffering is the idea that you exist. The idea that somehow you might avoid suffering by acting one way rather than another creates suffering.

Q: Is it suffering if one wants to be happy?

K: Of course! Even those who are happy have to fight for their happiness. After all, you always have the chance of misfortune, which alone makes happiness unhappy. As long as there's one who's happy, there also must be one who's unhappy, both within the same person. As long as there's one free of suffering, there's also one who suffers.

Nobody can escape this cycle. The only possibility is the so-called divine accident, the realization that there never was one who existed in time, that there's no time, and that what you are is prior to any idea of space and time, prior to any idea whatever.

Q: And is there nothing I can do for this?

K: You don't have to do anything! Whatever's done in space and time, for or against it, can't touch you. Whatever's done in space and time can't make you into what you are.

It's very simple. What you are simply realizes that it can't be anything it can realize. Within you, within your awareness, space, time, and the world appear, but you yourself are never part of it.

The Pearl Necklace of Your Personal History

Every moment is a pearl in an infinite heap,
where each one is dependent on the others.

Question: I suddenly find myself free of tension, which refused to leave me, although I tried many ways to be rid of it. Although I've done nothing, now it's gone. Is it because I let go or because I strived so hard before?

Karl: Whatever you could let go of or hold on to, whatever you could do or not do, has led to this. Every step toward this one point was the right step, and at the same time you never decided what step to take. Each step was the result of an infinite interrelation, since all things are conditionally related to one another. Every moment is a pearl in an infinite heap, where each one is dependent on the others.

Q: Perhaps it's a necklace of pearls.

K: The necklace is your personal history. But is the past essential for the future? Or is it just an interrelation in which everything exists simultaneously, never coming or going? A necklace is an individual string of pearls. You've selected some pearls and tied them together, one after the other, as personal moments. You hang the necklace around your neck and say, "My necklace ... my story ... my past ... my future ... my life!" Such a necklace is very heavy to wear!

Even the "I" finds it unbearable. That's why the "I" constantly tinkers with it, trying to make it more beautiful and delicate, trying to shine more brilliantly or perhaps more discreetly, so it appears less obvious!

Q: It does this until the "I" finally drops the necklace.
K: It's impossible for the "I" to drop it. It can't let go. The necklace is there because the "I" is there, and the "I" is there only because of the necklace. They're inseparable prerequisites for each other.

Q: Then there's only one possibility: They must both disappear simultaneously.
K: The only possibility is to realize that they never existed— neither the "I" nor the necklace.

Q: You mean that there's no personal history, no sequence of moments?
K: What you are is without sequence and condition. It's not divisible into moments, it's not part of anything, and it's always prior to everything.

Q: It's not even a heap of pearls?
K: It's prior to the heap of pearls and laughs when you trip on it.

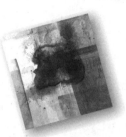

Good Company

Contact with existence doesn't exist. For that you would need two.

Question: Can meeting with spiritual people help my personal development?
Karl: Whatever develops can't be what you are as part of evolution. You can experience both personal development and the development of humankind. These exist as part of the play of thoughts. Can this drama make any difference when it comes to realizing who you are?

Q: Probably not.
K: Through such dramas you can realize what you're not. That's what they're good for—the absolute realization that you can't be what you realize. This understanding might give you some enjoyment.

Q: But I feel that I've developed. Ten years ago I didn't have the connection to existence that I have now.

K: You can never have a connection to existence. There are no connections to existence because there's no separation.

Q: What I meant to say is that years ago I had no contact with existence.

K: Contact with existence doesn't exist. For that you would need two. But there's no such thing as "my" existence and "your" existence. You could say that you observe a development from a more individual consciousness to a more cosmic consciousness.

Q: That's what I mean.

K: Then it is called *satori*, awakening, or enlightenment.

Q: That's what I mean. And don't these moments of awakening occur at certain specific points in one's development?

K: They come and go on their own. However, whatever wakes up can go to sleep again. Every "I" that disappears can reappear. There's no lack of opportunity for the ego to return. Therefore, you haven't gained any lasting advantage.

Q: Ramesh Balsekar says, "You walk up the stairs slowly, and then the last step occurs suddenly." He says quite clearly that there's a process of development.

K: Yes, there's a process, and this "legal" process is against you!

Q: Didn't you go through some development, too?

K: They initiated proceedings against Little Karl, as well. He sat in the dock as the accused and had to prove his existence, but he failed. Little Karl's inability to prove his existence has done away with him.

Q: How does one come before such a court?
K: It depends on the judge.

Q: And who's the judge?
K: It's the Self, which doesn't let anything pass except itself. The "I" has to prove that it exists, but it doesn't. Because of this, it may go a little crazy in its desperate desire for proof. We call the trial scene in which this occurs "The Last Judgment." It's the "last" judgment because at this moment time ceases to exist, and there's only beginning. It's the last day, the youngest day, in which only the source exists and only the source can exist. This is the Last Judgment of the Bible, in which whatever isn't the source is cancelled. Such a courtroom accepts no evidence that can exist in time.

Q: And you went through this process?
K: Proceedings were initiated against Little Karl and he was executed.

Q: Does this mean that relinquishing the "I" is painful?
K: The sentence is executed with a blunt sword or by slow hanging.

Q: Is it unpleasant in every case?
K: There are no rules. You're being hanged, but you don't know how long it will last until you're bled out until every desire and intention is gone. It's a hang-up. You're being hung up.

Q: One hangs from a rope and nobody cuts it?

K: At some point the cut occurs, which is salvation. Suddenly the one who's hanging there vanishes. You realize that it was you on whom everything was hanging and on whom everything depended.

You Don't Need to Change Anything

In this moment of clarity, there never was a "before" or "after." To be what you are, you don't need time.

Question: I have the feeling that I'm slowly beginning to wake up, more or less.

Karl: That's impossible! Since in this eternal Now there's only the experience of the pure Self, there's absolutely no sense of "more or less." There's no "closer" to it, "more advanced," "less advanced," or everything else. Nobody's enlightened or unenlightened; in fact, any idea of awakening disappears. There are no sleeping or awakened ones anymore, no more hocus-pocus of trying to get anywhere and have special experiences, or any other such nonsense.

Where I am, nobody can be. No one's awakened and no one's sleeping because that which exists has never slept and therefore never can awaken. Every personal awakening is a joke, a fart in the wind. A person can never wake up because the Self is always awake.

Q: You say it's nonsense if someone says he's realized or enlightened.

K: The only thing one can say is that there's no personal story anymore. One's history, which seemed so real before, drops away. A person can never say, "Now I'm enlightened."

Whatever happens in time can't make you into what you already are. The Self becoming aware of "it-Self" doesn't depend on the person. It occurs spontaneously, not because of some event in time.

Q: Is there still a person then?

K: Yes. For example, Ramana said, "As awareness, I am absolute awareness; as consciousness, I am absolute consciousness, and as man, I am absolute man." Jesus said the same thing: "I and my Father are one." When relativity is present, the Self is lost. That which lives the human being is this same ever-present existence.

Q: And am I an aspect of that?

K: An aspect is fleeting. Check whether you're something fleeting or something that is. An aspect is just an angle on something, only a passing reflection of what you are. You're the absolute manifesting itself as a human being, as the moon, the sun, and all the universe. You're reality itself. Whether you realize yourself as a human being, a stone, or a tree, you're the truth, the reality.

Q: Then I don't need to strive for enlightenment.

K: To "strive for enlightenment" means that an object thinks it can do something to bring about absolute existence. The object thinks it needs to change something, so the absolute state may come into being. In this way, what's perfect can become a bit more perfect! But when Ramana says, "Be what you are," it simply means, "Be this absolute existence, be that which you can't not be," and let the details follow their own destinies.

Q: But apparently you can work toward this moment when you can "be what you are."

K: Yes. Nisargadatta Maharaj said, "There were times in which I existed and thereby populated the world. Those were times in which I and human beings still existed. But since this one here exists no more, no population exists either. Since then, the world is empty." Thus, there were times in which he lived in the illusion that he existed as a separate being among other separate beings. He believed it, and although it may have been a dream, it appeared real to him.

After all, when you perceive an idea, it seems true. Only when you find out that it's false does the illusion burst. In this moment of clarity, there never was a "before" or "after." To be what you are, you don't need time.

Q: How does this help my daily life?

K: You simply see that there never was anyone who could change anything. When you see that your ordinary Self is perfection itself, you realize that this ordinariness is no more ordinary than the eternal NOW, which never comes or goes. Just look inside yourself for the vision of God. In Meister Eckhart's words, "The eye by which I see God is the same eye by which God sees me. My eye and God's eye are one and the same—one in seeing, one in knowing, and one in loving."

Q: Well, that's Meister Eckhart. I haven't had this realization.

K: You never had anything and never will have anything. But in the moment of this realization, you see that this is how it's always been. Then there's no more "before" or "after." And it's effortless! Nothing needs to be done, nothing needs to change, nothing has to go, and nothing has to come. It fact, nothing needs to be understood.

Q: Then I'm relieved.

K: Me, too!

There's Nothing to Surrender

*Realize that there's nothing to surrender
because there's nothing that you own.*

Question: Is it necessary to build up a certain quality of "I"?
Karl: You can blow it up, and people certainly do. But it's rather rare that it bursts.

Q: I don't mean that.
K: The ego is a hot air balloon, and every thought expands it.

Q: Do you need to be particularly strong or healthy to bear the awakening from the ego?
K: No, the ego can't be healthy. You may have psychological health, which means that your ego can adapt to various situations and live in harmony with its environment. This notion is debatable, but even if it were true, it has no significance. No ego can be healthy or strong enough to bear "I"-lessness.

Q: But can't the ego recognize how it obstructs the truth?

K: The ego never realizes anything, but is part of what's realized. The ego never understands anything; only the whole, the Self, understands. No "I" ever understands anything.

Q: But can't I understand the reasons for suffering? Can't I analyze it or witness it and see that I'm not the suffering?

K: Whatever you do with the ego results in fumbling about, which is the attempt to control things. Whether you want to endure suffering without being touched by it, or whether you enter completely into it, every technique you use results in your controlling it. And this doesn't just apply to suffering; you want to control the whole of existence! You want existence to touch you only as far as you allow it. And to top it off, God, who controls the state of the world, is then supposed to wake up inside you.

Q: In my experience, the acceptance of suffering is like devotion or praying.

K: As long as you think you have an advantage from acceptance, devotion, or prayer, the controller, the "I," stays alive, and as long as he lives, everything is suffering. The "I" creates the pain of separation, the pain of longing for what you are—the Absolute One free from a second. But the idea that you need to control something to be free allows the small, separate "I" to remain.

Even if you surrender, it, too, is an attempt to control things. You expect this "surrender" to make everything more beautiful for you. But what we're talking about is surrendering the surrender. Realize that there's nothing to surrender because there's nothing that you own.

Q: Can't I even control whether my eating is healthy?

K: The idea that you control something always comes after the event. Whatever happens, happens on its own. Afterward, you believe that you did it, but in truth it didn't happen through you. The idea simply appears that you act and that you have the power to control things. Such an idea belongs to the "my," the illusion that there's something belonging to you—an action, a mind, a body. You feel that you're the owner who wants to control what he owns, but nothing belongs to him. He owns nothing. He doesn't even exist.

Q: To believe this is absurd. I wonder what's happening here.

K: Everything just becomes more confused and chaotic.

Q: As far as I'm concerned, I can only say that something surrenders.

K: One can say that something removes itself from the objects, which is Jesus' idea of deliverance. He is the redeemer who removes you from worldly objects and leads you to objectlessness. What you are frees itself from everything that can be realized and known and becomes a mystery.

Mystery means complete unknowing, without any object that you can know. But you can never reach this mystery, lose it, or surrender to it.

It Simply Happens

You have a simple "aha"-realization that you've always been what you are and always will be.

Question: A few years ago, I suddenly knew that there's nothing to do. It was there, crystal clear, but only for a few days, after which this clarity left. Now occasionally I plan not to do anything, but soon I'm doing something again. So what is this so-called "doing in non-doing?"
Karl: Who does something?

Q: That's what I'm asking you.
K: Who does everything?

Q: They used to say God.
K: Does anything ever happen at all?

Q: Yes, I do have that impression.
K: Is something happening now?

Q: I would say so.

K: And is someone necessary who experiences this as an event?

Q: If you ask me in this way, I'd say probably not. Intellectually, I also know that there's no doer. But what use is that to me?

K: Knowledge doesn't bring a solution. Relative knowledge, which is all an "I" can have, will never free that "I" from separation because there will always be the need for somebody to own the knowledge. As long as there's someone who knows, separation exists. You may have the highest knowledge of the most subtle experience, but it still won't bring deliverance. As long as there's still one who knows, separation remains. Where there's absolute knowledge, there's no one left to own it.

Q: But each of us wants cosmic consciousness.

K: Whether one speaks of individual or cosmic consciousness, some "thing" always desires the absolute bliss of pure existence. The individual consciousness strives to transform itself to reach cosmic consciousness. But cosmic consciousness can easily slip back to individual consciousness. What I'm talking about is prior to consciousness, an awareness in which nobody can exist to be aware of herself or himself and where awareness is everything. Awareness is prior to consciousness and relative knowledge.

Q: When can I experience this? When does it happen?

K: It's a totally spontaneous non-event that never happens.

Q: It comes on its own?

K: It happens with or without effort. It comes in spite of, not because of effort or its absence.

Q: When does it happen? Does it occur sometime or other according to its own discretion?

K: It has nothing to do with what exists in time. It involves the simple realization that "you" are prior to time. You realize that time awakens within "you" and not you within time. It's like a magnetic field that flips: Suddenly time is within you; and you're no longer within time. Time only reflects what you are, and there's no more doing. You have a simple "aha"-realization that you've always been what you are and always will be. Whatever exists in time is nothing but a fleeting shadow.

Q: Is there no more doing, only realization?

K: There's also no more realization. In this moment the one who realizes, the realizing, and what's realized are all one without separation.

Q: Then does one simply witness everything in the waking, dream, and deep sleep states?

K: A witness still makes distinctions. I talk about that which never makes any distinctions and for whom no differences exist. Whatever it may be is what it is. In whatever state, it always remains what it is. It's neither this nor that. It's not witness consciousness, an observer, or an individual person. The three states of waking, dream, and deep sleep appear within that which it is. The witness state, however, is still about an event, something that happens or doesn't. What I speak about can never happen and can't be defined. For this, nothing needs to be done. Indeed, there's nothing that can be done.

Q: That's really mean. We can neither wait, hope, or do anything else.
K: On the contrary, you can do everything.

Q: Frankly speaking, we're sitting here so that it can happen—and as soon as possible.
K: Your sitting here will neither help nor prevent it. Since there's no causality, what you're waiting for won't happen for any reason. If it's supposed to happen, it will. You can do or not do whatever you like. No action of yours can obstruct or hasten it.

Q: But it will happen, won't it?
K: Let me give you an official guarantee: Its happening is unavoidable.

Q: Will it happen in this life?
K: It's unimportant in which life it happens, since no life exists in this.

Q: What?
K: It knows no life. The Self is aware of itself and is pure Self-awareness. You don't need time for this realization. Its nature has never been hidden, and it's nothing new. Actually, there's no such thing as awakening.

Q: There's no awakening?

K: Whatever can wake up is within consciousness. The individual consciousness can wake to cosmic consciousness and fall asleep again. But the Self is never asleep or awake. It knows neither sleeping nor waking. It always is what it is and knows no states.

Q: But what about you? Do you still experience different states?
K: I don't talk about what I am. I will never be able to define myself or realize myself.

I will never know what I am. But I know with one hundred percent certainty that I am. I also know that whatever comes and goes as appearance or information in any state exists because I am. It's not that I am because something appears. I am the primordial ground in which everything happens.

Q: Do you feel that you're the source of everything?
K: I'm not the source. The source is also nothing but a state.

Q: Is there some kind of creator God?
K: I am prior to the creator, prior to God. What I am in essence is prior to everything. When Jesus says, "I and the Father are one, but I am not the Father," he means that God in his role as creator, Jesus as a human being, and the indefinable Holy Spirit are one in essence, although different in form. Therefore, the creator God is still different from the essence. In the Hindu system, Brahma, too, is not the same as the essence. The Indians call it *Parabrahma*, that which exists *para* (prior to) God. One can never define it, yet one can talk about it forever. One can never grasp it or

make it into an object. It's incomprehensible, unfathomable, and beyond definition.

Q: Are there still times when you identify with a thought or a feeling?

K: Whether identified or not identified, it makes no difference to me. Both appear as fleeting sensations. The identified consciousness and the cosmic consciousness are both aspects of me, yet I am prior to both, prior to whatever can be described, prior to everything, identifiable or not. This unmanifest consciousness is sometimes called "the noumenon." It simply is.

Q: Is this state more natural than the one we're in?

K: All states are natural states. None is more natural and clear, or less natural and more foggy.

A little "aha" reveals the essence, which is prior to all origins and birth, and which exists throughout all time. It's never foggy and never will be. It's never touched by anything that exists in time.

Q: Maybe the essence isn't, but I am! Isn't there a body here and a world out there?

K: The body and the world appear together with the "I"-thought. From the pure consciousness, "I am," the totality of manifestation rises like a huge tree. Everything appears out of "I am." But prior to "I am" there is "I-I," which is always there and which remains untouched by ideas like "I am this or that" or "I am here while the world is out there." Nothing can cloud it.

Q: But why am I caught in this fixation on "I" and the world?

K: It's unimportant. This fixation can do nothing to what you are. Personal consciousness, which identifies with the body, is no worse than cosmic consciousness. There's no difference in quality. What you really are doesn't differentiate between personal and cosmic points of view.

Q: I would prefer the cosmic point of view.

K: Every thought that there's something other than you creates separation. All the so-called nondual teachings of *Advaita* inform you that only the one Self exists and nothing else.

Q: Maybe so, but I don't experience it.

K: Every experience is Self-experience. The Self only knows itself. Even personal experience is pure Self-experience. There is only the Self, the foundation of what is. Even if it shows itself as the world, whatever appears is the Self, which is never disturbed by anything and always One without a second.

Love and Partnership

Where there's no more "you and others,"
there's only love. Everyone desires this love;
it's the true meaning of relationship.

Question: Right now I'm in love. I love someone—not pure being or the Self—but another person. Is this allowed?
Karl: No, it's strictly prohibited!

Q: Does loving another qualify as love? Is it real love?
K: There are countless books and sayings about this thing called "love." You'll find more definitions in them than there are people in the world.

Q: Don't you have one?
K: I only know that where there's a concept about it, love is absent.

Q: What?
K: Love can exist only where there's no concept of "love." As

long as it's limited by a concept, it's imprisoned. You want to define love, and the word "define" literally means "to limit." Your desire to define love this way or that way turns it into your possession, a love you have at your disposal, a love that has an owner. Love that's thus limited and imprisoned certainly isn't the infinite love that everyone longs for.

Q: But isn't there a love that isn't imprisoned?
K: There is. It exists where there's nobody who could own love. This love is freedom, and only this is love. Love is the absence of a person who defines true love this way or another. Love is the absence of one who discriminates.

Q: Well, I guess this has nothing to do with my being in love.
K: There's no such thing as "your" love. Love knows no owner. Where "my" and "your" stop, love begins.

Q: Then love can't be an emotion.
K: Love is all emotions because it's the source and essence of everything.

Q: Do you also approve of personal love, the spontaneous love that's directed at a particular human being?
K: When you recognize yourself completely in others and when there's no more separation between you and them, there's love. Then love is synonymous with Self-realization. You realize that what you are is also what the other being is. Where there's no more "you and others," there's only love. Everyone desires this love; it's the true meaning of relationship.

Q: Yes, and love may also come within relationships.

K: It comes and goes again. This taste of love is temporary—and fatal! Love in this form is fleeting and it hurts. Even when such love arrives, you know it's going to leave again because it's subject to time.

Q: Always?
K: Without exception. Whatever comes in time goes in time. But the source of relative love, Love itself, is always there.

Q: But suppose a relationship that you call "relative love" is built on Love.
K: Then we can work on it to make it last forever—or at least until death! We only need to give it total commitment! Yes, work and dedication! But is there someone who needs this relative love? Who needs this emotion, this care and security, to exist or to be happy?

Q: Well, that one does exist, and he's sitting here.
K: When love comes face to face with need, need always wins.

Q: What if it isn't like that in a particular relationship?
K: Then there's no relationship; it simply ends.

Q: Do you mean that if I'm love, I can't relate to someone else?
K: Yes, because there's no more two-ness: no more you and someone else. With this Love, relationship ends, and compassion flowers, although no one exists to have this compassion.

Q: It sounds lonely.

K: Love is ultimate loneliness because there's no more two-ness. You are That, One without a second. At this moment, everything that's in time has to die, including you as a separate person who can't exist in this loneliness.

Q: It sounds terrible.
K: For a person nothing is more terrifying. Any person would commit suicide just to avoid it!

Q: But isn't there an emotion called love?
K: One may call it that, but it's not love. Whatever can be named isn't It. You can have a nice sensation that comes and goes, like the taste of a good meal or the feeling of harmony. Just as these sensations pass, so does fleeting love, which will never make you content.

Q: That's why we want eternal love.
K: We want it so we're totally safe!

Q: We want this feeling never to stop.
K: Love exists when the idea drops that someone wants or needs something. What you are is itself already eternity, and therefore has no need of any feeling or idea of the "eternal." Love is not a feeling.

Q: Does your girlfriend hear this kind of confession of love from you?
K: If you'd ask her, she'd say she's never heard one. It's not relationship-heaven for her, yet all our interactions are testimonies of love.

Q: Does this reflect the saying, "No matter what I do, I am love"?

K: For me, love is one name among many. If you want to use this term, then that which I am is that which is love. I am not love; I am that which is love. That is whatever it is—the eternal mystery of existence.

Q: Then it's everybody.

K: Of course.

Q: But do you also experience something like the need for love?

K: That's called being a person, and I know this experience.

Q: But it doesn't affect you because you're rooted in existence?

K: That which I am, in essence, is never rooted or uprooted. It knows none of these definitions. It's that which never cares about anything.

Q: So the essence, love, never cares about anything?

K: It is completely care-less. The caring takes care.

Q: I never would have thought that of love.

K: That's why you have grief.

Is One Better Off Without Relationships?

The idea that you're separate from yourself is as crazy as the idea that you're separate from others.

Question: Jesus supposedly said, "Love others as yourself." Is this possible?

Karl: Nothing else is possible; it doesn't work otherwise. Love arises when you recognize yourself in everything. Then there's no more duality and no more need to make an effort to love someone you don't like, since love is a self-evident reality. Love is the recognition of yourself in others. Love doesn't come by thinking, "The essence of this person here in the subway is actually the same as mine, and therefore I'll say, 'Hello over there!'" You realize love spontaneously; it's what you are. That's why love and self-realization are one and the same.

On the entry to the temple in Delphi, where it was written "Know yourself," it could equally have read, "Love yourself," but perhaps that would have had an undesirable effect on the priests!

Q: To "know yourself" give better access to the Self.

K: There's no access to it and simply no way out of it. You can't become what you are through devotion or the process of becoming. The idea that you're separate from yourself is as crazy as the idea that you're separate from others. You're not separate from yourself, but if you believe you are, then in your thoughts you build a "relationship" with yourself, one that you can work on regularly, since it certainly needs improvement!

Essentially, you operate as if there were a second self. Out of a sense of unity, you imagine two-ness, although in reality this separation doesn't exist. But if you believe in relationships and the need to relate to someone, then you believe in the idea of separation.

Q: Then is it better to have no relationships at all?

K: It's better when there's nobody who could have a relationship.

Q: Well, I have one, but I can't really call it love. It's difficult for me to say to a woman, "I love you." Is it because of an inability to love or the feeling that these three words contain a relationship that limits true love?

K: It's more the fear of committing yourself to something that might make you suffer.

Q: So it's lovelessness, after all!

K: It's the fear that it could turn into lovelessness. Hence, you don't want to commit to anything. If you give yourself completely, you'll lose yourself in the other.

Q: So should I dare to jump and say, "I love you"?

K: It can't happen through words, although words can express it. If they're there, they're there. Surrendering yourself happens when it happens. Devotion (*bhakti*) or realization happens when it happens. They can't be created.

Q: Even when I'm carried away, I never say, "I love you."

K: You're afraid that you'll be taken at your word. You find this intimate confession really difficult because behind it lurks the fear of losing yourself.

Q: That's a clear answer.

K: Ultimately, this fear of losing oneself is the reason why people build defensive walls. It's an attempt at self-protection. But I can lose something only if I first believe that it's mine—"my" life, "my" body, "my" world, "my" personal concept of love. The very idea that I own something (whether it be "my" knowledge, "my" body, or "my" life) demands security and protection, which create controls and locked doors. "I love you" opens them all up.

Q: And in front of this, I tremble.

K: Yes, perhaps nothing will remain of you, nothing of the identity that you believe is yours.

Q: But once I speak these words, I imagine that I'll find myself amazingly relaxed.

K: You'll feel relaxed when you don't have to maintain anything anymore—no identity, stories, or future. When you're simply that which is, when there's no more "two" and hence no relationship, then all tension disappears.

Q: I'll have no more tension?

K: You'll have nothing tense, nothing pulling and pinching at you anymore.

Q: The lack of friction, excitement, and sex would create a problem for me.

K: You have this problem already. Right now you're creating it for yourself. When you consider the "I" to be real, at that very moment it is. If you think this relationship problem and your body exist, then they do.

Q: I simply have to stick to my subject: How real is sex?

K: It's as real as you want it to be.

Q: Thank God!

K: Every sexual act is masturbation, with the aim of reaching the orgiastic feeling of "I"-lessness.

Q: At least a relationship is good for this!

K: Whatever you do is masturbation until the cosmic orgasm occurs, which is called enlightenment. Then you explode. Everything aims at this cosmic Big Bang, which never has a beginning and in which nothing exists anymore.

Q: How wonderful! That's good! That's how I'll explain it to my girlfriend.

K: You could also try saying, "I love you."

Searching and Longing

Can one thing really unite with another?
Can one thing split into two?"

Question: I'm full of longing, although I don't know what for.

Karl: Longing appears when you think you've lost something, such as the aliveness of your childhood. You may experience longing when you want to move somewhere else—to another environment, for example. Longing may also appear when you imagine conditions that might make you feel better, such as a harmonious relationship, a good job, financial security, a happy family, or sound health. Generally, longing arises when you'd like to have a situation that you don't presently have, or at least think you don't. Then you search for something that seems missing or lost.

Q: I see. Isn't the search for happiness our basic longing? This search is programmed deep inside our cells.

K: Whatever's in time longs for timelessness. Whatever's separate wants to return to it source in unity. The idea of duality always contains the longing for unity.

Q: My longing is not an idea; it's a deep feeling!
K: It arises from the illusion of incompleteness, from the idea of an "I." As soon as the "I"-thought arises, there comes the longing for "I"-lessness, for desirelessness. Thus, there promptly appears the longing to be free of all longing. What's separated must be joined; the two must become one.

Q: Of course! It's the longing to be free from desires, free from time! To live like that, completely content in the moment, must be happiness. Is it wrong to search for this? You act as if it's a mistake. What's going on?
K: I grew up on a farm. If someone asked, "What's going on here?" there was always one answer: "Whatever's not held back is going on." That doesn't explain anything, but it's a logical answer. The question is not what's going on or what's held back, but "Is there anything at all that could be held back?"

Q: That's what you talked about on your farm?
K: And for this we squandered our European Community subsidy! We asked ourselves, "Can one thing be held back by another separate thing? Can there really be two, with one holding back another? Can one thing really unite with another? Can one thing split into two?"

Q: It sounds like ecological farming! What result did you arrive at?

K: I saw that to be connected and to be separate are both illusions because nothing can be removed from something else and nothing can be connected to something else.

Q: You call that agricultural economy?
K: I call it Self-realization.

Q: I would say it's self-repression.
K: As long as you hold the idea of being connected or separate, you long to change the situation and find a way back to the source, to unity, to the Self. This longing makes you a so-called seeker, an addict, addicted to your-self, self-ish! Every seeker is self-addicted.

Q: Is there a way to either cure or satisfy this addiction?
K: You don't have to fulfill or remove this longing.

Q: Is that how I can live in peace?
K: What you are is prior to any kind of peace or conflict. You're prior to every sensation, perception, or concept. Everything appears and disappears within you. Longing and seeking are part of these appearances, too. You don't need the fulfillment of any kind of seeking to be what you are. For this, nothing has to come and nothing has to go. You yourself are the fulfillment you seek.

Q: I don't have that impression.
K: You're complete, with or without your longing. With or without seeking, what you are is absolute and eternally complete in itself. Therefore, nothing has to be changed, and nothing has to happen. Nothing needs to be avoided; for you

to be what you are, nothing has to come, and nothing has to go.

Q: Yes, but I would like to have this realization myself, or at least to rediscover it.

K: The desire to rediscover it comes from the crazy idea that you've lost it, but there's never been a moment when you weren't there. The entire falseness of seeking comes from this mistake. You have nothing to gain or find again. This perfect existence, which is right here, is the basis for every appearance, for every question and answer. One doesn't have to do anything to realize this.

Q: Except be here!

K: Only be here in this absolute stillness. Realize that you never have any kind of need. What you are is never disturbed by anything that comes or goes, by any question or answer. Nothing can touch it; nothing can hide or reveal it. What you are is absolutely pure and always clear.

Q: Wow!

K: Nothing is held back. Nothing is going on.

Q: Like on your farm?

K: Like on a farm with its agricultural subsidies!

Happiness in Partnership

In emptiness there's a feeling of complete acceptance, which is comparable to love.

Question: Nondual teachers sometimes maintain that there are no relationships. Is this your experience?

Karl: What you really are has no relationships. In the dreamlike world, however, there are all kinds of relationships. But the essential point is that no one has them.

There are relationships between objects, and as long as you believe that this kind of "objectivity" is your reality, you're in a relationship. Ultimately, relationships don't exist.

Q: Doesn't the girlfriend of a satsang teacher live in a relationship?

K: The idea that there's another with whom you could have a relationship comes from the idea that you exist as a separate being. If that drops away, the idea of a relationship continues to exist as an idea, but no longer has any reality.

Q: In the old days, one would have talked about "love." Is that also just a concept?

K: If the love you talk about were possible, there would have to be two Selfs. In that case, love would be the love of the Self for a separate object; such a concept comes out of duality and eventually drops away. All "love" is really Self-love, since there's only the Self.

Q: Is there no love at all? Robert Adams said, "Everything is empty, yet love fills all of existence."

K: This kind of love arises only in absence of someone who accepts or doesn't accept. In emptiness there's a feeling of complete acceptance, which is comparable to love. If there's nothing left to accept, the one who has a need to accept has also disappeared. Thus, there's an absolute acceptance, which could be called love. But who needs this relationship? If it's defined as love, there must be something else that's not love. Immediately, an opposite is created.

The essence of love doesn't need love in order to exist.

Q: If the one who accepts drops away, does the one who wants to be accepted disappear at the same time?

K: Both disappear simultaneously. If you are what you are, all longing drops. There's no more desire for acceptance and harmony. There is peace because you're absent. Peace exists only when someone who needs peace is no longer there. As long as you exist as someone who craves peace, you're at war. You wage war for the sake of peace.

Q: You said that the longing drops . . .

K: You abide as you are, with or without longing, and you don't need the longing to drop away. Various forms of longing may still be there, but no one has the longing.

Q: What is longing without someone to have it?
K: There's a vibration of energy called "longing," but it doesn't mean anything anymore.

Q: But can't the longing serve a purpose in persuading us to strive toward the truth?
K: That's its origin. The moment you have the "I"-idea inside you, you long for what you are prior to the "I" idea. As a seed, longing urges you to find your way back to what you are. Only when you are what you are does the longing end. Whatever you do based on belief in existence and consciousness perpetuates the search for what's prior to consciousness. All science and religion arise from this longing.

Q: If longing drives me on, when will I find what I'm looking for?
K: You'll never find it. The longing for yourself will never find its fulfillment. You'll never find yourself. The search for yourself, which is based on longing, will never bring you to the goal. It's not intended to because there's no finder. Nobody ever finds anything. The longing simply stops, not because you find something, but rather because the longing gets lost.

Q: What's helpful in all this?
K: Nothing at all. The one who's longing at some point simply dissolves on its own. It came on its own, and all alone it'll go. One person can search and meditate for a thousand years and nothing will happen. Someone else just starts and boom!

It happens. There are no rules.

Q: And there's no justice, either.

K: If it were possible to get there by meditating, you could control freedom, which means it wouldn't be truly free. You can neither control nor attain the real freedom, which is the origin of your nature. Actually, through meditation you may achieve a certain harmony, but it remains temporary and vulnerable. As soon your tolerance reaches its limit, your harmony collapses.

Q: What if harmony increases?

K: Whatever can be brought into harmony at some time will return to disharmony. This isn't about the feeling of temporary happiness that can be attained through effort. It's not about the happiness of a person who buys a new Mercedes and is happy for a few hours or days until he finds the first scratch. It's not about the happiness that you dream will come from a beautiful house that suits you perfectly. The neighbors are already waiting to ensure that you won't find contentment! And if you have any doubts about this, death is waiting to knock on your door.

Q: But there are happy partnerships.

K: In a partnership you feel free for a while. Then it becomes a relationship and starts to pull and pinch. Partnerships can make you content within a harmonious environment, but this contentment is unstable and temporary. It doesn't fulfill the real aim of your longing, which concerns your true nature beyond all relationships and which is effortless, blissful happiness itself.

All Paths Lead to Love

If you need to exert effort to love another, such
"love" remains a concept and breeds suffering.

Question: Does passion disappear when one is enlightened?
Karl: When one is enlightened, I can guarantee that one will become endarkened again. And in this process, love is especially dangerous. One might say, "I had just became truly comfortable and established in my enlightenment when this incredibly hunky postman walked up my drive!" or "You should see this amazing woman who just moved in next door!"

Q: Seriously, shouldn't awakening free one from personal passions?
K: Whatever it "should" be isn't what it is. But when one gets rid of love, passion also goes.

Q: When one gets rid of love?
K: Yes, the end of love brings the end of suffering and passion.

Q: You mean the end of personal love?

K: The end of duality is where love really exists. Here there's no self that loves or doesn't love anything. Suffering ends because it's the end of the sufferer. As long as there's an "I" that loves itself or something else, suffering and passion arise. The love for yourself is the beginning of this suffering.

Q: But one should love oneself!

K: That's the beginning of everything. To love yourself means there's a Self that looks at itself as an object for love. This in itself is already duality. The love of the Self for itself is the root of all suffering.

Q: One of your predecessors once said, "Love your neighbor as yourself"!

K: Who is that supposed to be?

Q: I've heard that when you love yourself, you can build a bridge to others, which dissolves duality.

K: As long as there's a someone who loves something else, that love is directed toward objects and is rooted in duality. If you need to exert effort to love another, such "love" remains a concept and breeds suffering.

Q: What do you mean by effort? In India one simply says, *Namaste*: "I recognize myself in you."

K: If you want to recognize yourself in another so you can love him as yourself, you must make an effort to recognize this condition.

Q: Can't love be completely effortless?

K: I can't remember.

Q: I'm talking about love that arises spontaneously, that manifests in the mirror of another, and that manifests simply and immediately.

K: When you're that which is love, effort no longer exists. Nobody's left who loves or doesn't love. There's only freedom: the freedom of love and freedom from the idea of love. In a sense, what remains is loveless love, the love that gets rid of you. But as long as you have an idea of love; as long as you think you should love yourself in others or others in yourself; as long as you think that love should be a bridge and dissolve duality or that it needs to be spontaneous, you'll suffer. Love based on an idea of love is full of suffering. This love creates suffering.

Q: When love unites the lover with the beloved, there's happiness.

K: As soon as you take the first step outside the paradise of "I"-lessness, a longing arises to find the way back. You'll do anything to find your way back and merge. And every step is right. As long as there are steps, there are only right steps. You can do whatever you want. All paths lead to love.

Q: So that's why people love. How wonderful!

K: Love doesn't need to love. It doesn't need an object. It doesn't need you or your ideas. But in some moments you simply forget them. You even forget love. Then you are what love is, self-forgetfulness that's prior to duality. But you can't "do" this. Every desire to forget yourself is based on the memory of yourself. Love can only happen spontaneously, and then time and separateness cease. Then you're what love is, no matter what happens, even if nothing happens. And perhaps nothing does happen. Love doesn't need to love in order to be love.

Pain and Laughing Gas

The fundamental cure involves being prior to consciousness and time.

Question: Obviously, there's suffering. In truth, it may be a dream or illusion, but for the one who's suffering it's not.
Karl: The Self doesn't experience suffering as suffering. In Self-realization, suffering is no less blissful than joy. Suffering and joy aren't separate.

Q: It doesn't get me anywhere when you explain it this way intellectually.
K: The intellect is meant to separate. It separates between joy and suffering, between good and bad experiences. But that which created the intellect, the essence of the intellect, no longer distinguishes suffering from joy.

Q: Well, I'd like to see that person who has severe pain and smiles blissfully at it.

K: The basic point is that there's no experiencer! The one who experiences, the experiencing, and that which is experienced appear together as one. As long as you identify with the one who experiences, you remain separate from the experiencing and the experience.

Q: Is there a right way to avoid making that identification?
K: Every drug experience shows you how to do this. You take morphine so that awareness can remove itself from identification with the body. In that removal from identification, the pain stops. When I was five years old, I got laughing gas at the dentist. Immediately, I was outside the body and watched how the dentist pulled my teeth. I was totally fascinated: I had no more pain, and consciousness was free in space!

Q: But when the effect subsides . . .
K: Then the pain immediately reappears. There's no escape.

Q: That's what I mean; pain can't be denied.
K: If there's one who can have pain, then pain is generated.

Q: So when there's a body, pain arises?
K: No, pain arises with the idea that I have pain.

Q: And you don't have this idea? If I stab a knife into your arm . . .
K: Then there's the sensation of pain. At that moment there's pain.

Q: I'm glad you admit it.
K: At that moment there's a complete experience of pain.

Shortly afterward the experience leaves. There's nobody left who holds on to the pain as an experience in time, who retains the "my-pain experience" of five minutes ago or the experience of a year ago. They may still be there as a memory, but there's nobody left to say, "That was my pain."

Q: But you just said it.
K: Not really. The speaking speaks on its own. The speaking speaks, but there's no "my" speaking. I've never said anything.

Q: And how are you now?
K: I'm as always. Even if you asked me in death, I would say, "As always." What I am is always there. That's why I can only say, "I'm as always."

Q: You've made one slight improvement: You're no longer dependent on laughing gas.
K: Oh, I made a lot of effort to get laughing gas. My mother warned me that if I ate too many sweets, I would have to go to the dentist. I was ecstatic. I was the only one in my class who loved to go to the dentist!

One person has an experience that makes him enter Hell, while another finds the exact same experience enables him to escape it. It's like the case of someone whose pain becomes so strong that he can't stand it anymore, so he leaves the pain.

Q: He becomes unconscious.
K: And "unconscious" means that consciousness separates itself from the body. You're still conscious, but you're simply

-111-

no longer inside the body. You can no longer be defined. When you come to the point that you can't stand it anymore, consciousness removes itself spontaneously.

Q: It's done by the unconscious.

K: "Done" isn't the right word. When it becomes unbearable, consciousness removes itself, not because someone has "done" something to make it happen, but because it's simply unbearable. At that point the individual consciousness disconnects itself and dissolves into cosmic consciousness because the Hell of separateness is unbearable.

Q: Does this disconnection lead to healing?

K: No, it doesn't confer such an advantage. What can be disconnected can also connect again. Whatever can go into unity can also return to duality. You come from the idea of duality into unity, cosmic consciousness, nothingness. You're the center of the universe, the consciousness that penetrates itself.

I went through all this and saw that I had gained nothing. What I was in essence was still exactly the same as before. Whether "I" am as "I"-consciousness or as cosmic consciousness, I'm neither of these.

Consciousness, which depends on time, reflects my existence. Every pain and experience is part of consciousness. The fundamental cure involves being prior to consciousness and time.

My Body, My Pain

You're not afraid of death, but you simply don't want to be there when death comes.

Question: While I sit here, somewhere in the world people are being murdered. What do you have to say about that? It's not okay, is it?

Karl: For whom isn't it okay?

Q: It's not okay for me, and I can guarantee it's not for the people who are being murdered.

K: Can you guarantee that?

Q: Well, it's simply a principle of life. After all, we're here to live and not to be murdered.

K: Life itself kills you. Whether in the form of another person, a tree next to the road, or a function within the body, life always kills life. But the only thing that dies is an idea while the essence remains. What you are remains while only the unreal disappears. Consciousness remains; it plays as the tree, another person, the culprit and the victim, and whatever appears.

Q: Anyway, I'd prefer to die a natural death.
K: You're not afraid of death, but you simply don't want to be there when death comes. There's no natural death because nothing dies. Your essence is the only thing alive and that's immortal. It was never born and has no form that can die. However, what you call life was never alive.

Q: And it doesn't live even now! Do I sit here as a corpse?
K: We should investigate that. Let's investigate where the idea originates that "This is my body." A baby can't say it, doesn't feel it, and doesn't think about it, either. But it begins in about the third year after the parents have incessantly repeated, "You're Little Karl, my Little Karl, that's who you are!"

Until then, Little Karl didn't even know it existed. When it could speak, it first said, in the third person, "Little Karl wants to drink; Little Karl has broken this; Little Karl is good." The identification of an "I" with the body hadn't become a reality yet. But eventually, it said, "This is me. This is my hand and my foot," and it began to feel responsible for itself.

Q: If the identification with the body is a mistake that was drummed into me, can I free myself from it?
K: Who has to free himself from it?

Q: Me, of course. Someone else can't.
K: And who is this "me"?

Q: It's the one who feels the body. If someone inflicts pain on me, it hurts me.

K: Then you have a phenomenon of pain.

Q: You could call it that. I simply have pain, and I don't like it.

K: Well, consciousness receives information about the pain and reacts to it. Nothing is wrong with that. Without the idea that it's "your" reaction and "your" pain, it's simply a play of energies.

Q: It doesn't feel like play. I certainly have the idea that it's my pain!

K: To free you from this dilemma, you have to realize that what you are is prior to the idea of a body.

Q: I want to get out of this dilemma. How can I realize this for myself?

K: Just see you're that which realizes and not anything that can be realized. Whatever you can realize is an object, so you can't be that. Neither can you be the one who jumps out of bed in the morning or who wakes up as the "I"-idea inside a body because he, too, is an object of perception, something that you can realize. However, you're always that which realizes, never something that can be realized.

Q: Yes, but that's precisely what I don't realize!

K: This realization, this perception that you are, simply exists. And in this perception, someone appears who asks the question, but he himself is merely an object. He can't realize what you are, and he doesn't have to. The perception that you are has always been there. The perception, within which all this appears and which is pure and clear in itself, is your reality, which one calls the eye of God.

Q: It sounds good, but I don't get it. Are you saying that whatever I see as alive really isn't?

K: Everything appears in perception and thus depends on there being a perceiver. It doesn't have separate existence, being merely an appearance.

Q: Is it, therefore, less real?

K: Perception is real. Awareness is real. What appears in it is just an appearance, such as nice weather and bad weather, beloved and enemy, victim and culprit, euphoria and loneliness, bankruptcy and lottery prizes, shaking hands and shaking in terror, peace and war.

Q: To take the most harmless example, in bad weather I get wet.

K: As long as you think that you're a being who was born and who is attached to a body, an individual being in this world separate from other beings who can affect you, you're at war with this world, and even at war with yourself. You always fear that something could happen to you, and because of this fear, you want to gain security and advantage over others. To protect yourself, you're prepared to harm somebody else, and, if necessary, to murder someone. You act out of fear that there are other beings and a hostile environment outside yourself.

Q: How can I realize that I'm not an individual being stuck in a body?

K: Turn the awareness towards awareness, not towards the phenomena that wander, ghostlike, in front of your outer and inner eyes. Don't turn toward what appears in your awareness, but toward awareness itself.

Q: If that's the case, I won't listen to you any longer because you, too, are merely an appearance in my awareness.
K: You don't listen to me anyway. If you listen at all, it's to yourself.

Q: So I gave the ten-Euro entrance fee to myself!
K: Correct! And it gets even clearer if you give fifty Euros! Try it out. Improve yourself slowly until enlightenment happens.

Q: Doesn't enlightenment happen when I empty myself completely?
K: Please don't empty yourself completely, here and now! Seriously, you're not the body that gives or takes, and not the intellect that hopes or regrets.

You become aware of these things, but awareness was already present before anything appeared in it. And whether you call this awareness, wakefulness, or attentiveness, it's what you are. Before a body awakes in the morning and an "I" makes itself felt and notices that "I am this" or "I have to do that," prior to this moment awareness is already there. And the famous question "Who am I?" aims exactly at what precedes everything else, what's prior to the "I" and any object of awareness.

In this way, awareness is directed toward the unfathomable mystery of being, which you are. No natural or artificial death can affect this great expanse of being.

Q: Before we awake in the morning and the "I" appears, isn't there a gap in which truth is present in complete purity.
K: Do you mean it's present in this one gap?

Q: No, of course not. The truth is always present, but we probably have the best chance of seeing it at this time.
K: But "you" don't see it. If anything sees it, your alarm clock does. "This is the pure truth!" it thinks as it sees you sleeping. "This is enlightenment!" it says shortly before you wake up. But then it must ring, a twitching goes through your body, and bang!, enlightenment is gone. Instead, you're there.

Q: Every day it's the same disappointment?
K: Yes, but only for your alarm clock and your wife. What you are remains untouched.

Compassion and Irritation

Everything is as it is, perfect in its irrelevance.

Question: For an enlightened one, you talk quite a bit.
Karl: Do I talk too much for you?

Q: At the very least, it's confusing. Your words seem totally relaxed, but you shoot them out like a machine gun. I find this really irritating.
K: It's good that this irritates you. When the "I" is being irritated, there's good reason to celebrate. The more confused the "I" becomes, the more it separates from what you really are. Thus, you free yourself from attachment, which is the intended result.

Q: Well, thank you very much.
K: I don't talk to any person, but to existence, the Self.

Q: You don't talk to me as a person?

K: No, and that absolutely irritates the person, whose "I"-idea may be pushed into total rebellion with a complete "Grrrrr!"

Q: You want to see me as a beast.

K: The nakedness itself wants you to get naked! The desirelessness itself desires it. And when it wants this . . .

Q: . . . then the "I"-thought is compelled to go.

K: And there's no escape. But you can't will this. Because it exists in simplicity, has no intentions, and happens to you, this indeed causes the irritation! There's a simultaneity of relaxing and talking from this machine gun that wants nothing from you, and that's irritating. Normally, someone wants something from you. Someone wants you to learn something, get somewhere, or wake up. Thus, your life passes by, all based on the attitude that, "Something's wrong with you, and you must do something about it!" But you won't hear these words here because you're already that which you are. I don't need to do anything about it.

Q: So the irritation is intended.

K: There may be an intention, but nobody has it.

Q: Aha, but there's an intention. Perhaps something should be changed after all!

K: No.

Q: You see the world, but since nothing needs to be changed, you can relax. But is there no compassion?

K: There's only compassion.

Q: Oh, really!
K: There's compassion.

Q: With what consequence?
K: Without consequence.

Q: Then it's pointless.
K: Compassion has no intention. Compassion is simply compassion.

Q: But doesn't this compassion create the desire to reduce suffering?
K: No, there's no suffering in compassion.

Q: Why, then, do enlightened beings come into this world, such as the *bodhisattvas*, with their deep desire to liberate all beings from suffering? They don't perceive the world as something separate, and yet they desire to bring it liberation.
K: If you want to liberate something, you have to see it as imprisoned. However, that which sees imprisonment must be imprisoned itself. The *bodhisattva* idea is also a concept.

Q: For those who suffer, a *bodhisattva* is very real and has critical significance.
K: In the *Diamond Sutra*, the Buddha said, "There never was a Buddha who entered the world, nor will there ever be one to enter it. I preached for forty years and didn't say a word to anybody."

Everything is as it is, perfect in its irrelevance. This is freedom—the fact that nothing has significance. Whether the comedy develops this way or that way, whether a *bodhisattva* appears or not . . .

Q: In my view that makes a difference!
K: It makes absolutely no difference what you are.

Q: A *bodhisattva* opens my heart.
K: Good, but whether he does it with or without an anesthetic makes no difference to that which you are.

Only with You Is There War

*Where there's "my existence," there's also
"your existence." By the age of three, at the
very latest, war has been declared.*

Question: Would you say something about war?
Karl: War comes from wanting to get something. Private wars
and big wars both begin this way. You want to gain something, believing it will make you happier.

Q: What if I want to get inner peace?
K: You simply want to catch up with yourself, which is war.
Since you're always after yourself, you're at war, either a bit
behind or ahead of yourself. It starts from the first thought,
the "I"-thought, which causes separation through which a
warrior is born with the idea that he must control his
environment. Thus war is declared.

Q: Are you claiming that everyone who thinks "I" is a
warrior?

K: Every "I"-thought is a warlike thought. With the idea that you exist and that an existence belongs to you, which you call "my life," you need to defend something. Thus, war is born. Where there's "my existence" there's also "your existence." By the age of three, at the very latest, war has been declared.

Q: I've heard there are societies of Native Americans in which there's no "I"-thought, but a community with an impersonal "I," a group "I." Within the group there's no "mine" or "yours" and no possession.

K: Yet outside the group there are "the others," so separation and war still exist.

Generally, in Western individualistic society, the small "I" is always on its own. Within the family, war is an ever-present reality. Siblings are always fighting to get more love and attention. This war always starts with the idea that there's someone who needs something—an "I" that identifies with a body or consciousness that sees itself as separate from the whole and needs something, like a feeling of unity and safety. We're always fighting to get something—possessions, food, or attention.

Q: Then animal's are also at war, even without any idea of "I."

K: That's simply programmed behavior along with hunger, hunting, and eating. Animals have no thinking directed to the future or past. A hamster may be hoarding food, but it doesn't worry about survival. However, we don't know what he talks about with his wife each evening in the nest!

Q: Is it possible to create peace, with or without weapons?

K: There will never be peace in this world. As long as there's an idea of separation, as long as you exist, there will be no peace. Just the idea of "you" means that something else exists with which there can be no peace. At any time a harmonious situation can turn into a warlike condition. Every peaceful person can turn into a beast if his or her limit for tolerance is crossed.

The peaceful human being doesn't exist. There are only different limits of tolerance, depending on the fineness of the filters that control the level of aggression.

Q: They also control the strength of the desire to kill.

K: I grew up on a farm. When slaughtering pigs, I had to hold on to their curly tails so that the sausages would be straight. The mood was phenomenal, charged to the extreme with energy. There was a glow that one could actually see: light ascending out of the material body into space.

Q: Can killing, therefore, have something to do with intoxication?

K: Yes. In an extreme situation, such as killing, the ego isn't there any longer, so you no longer exist. At that moment, consciousness detaches from the physical. Thus, a benefit that you're supposed to get from alcohol and drugs also comes from the direct experience of "I"-lessness. Such transcendence doesn't have to be connected to killing. Many other extreme situations also trigger it, such as bungee-jumping, mountain climbing, long-distance running, and auto racing. The "I" disappears in these activities. These extreme situations are like a meditation technique, a means to dissolve the "I." All human beings are searching and striving for this dissolution.

Q: What happens if the "I" dissolves?

K: Separation ends and there's only unity. You don't exist anymore, and the absence of you is freedom. You long for this freedom; however, the moment you desire to have it, it's gone. As long as someone's there to have this desire, it's blocked.

Q: To be free from myself means to be free of any idea of "I."

K: Yes, and this means to be free of the idea that you were born and thus are mortal. You've simply disappeared. Consciousness without the "I" is entirely impersonal. This feeling of unity is orgiastic.

Q: Do thoughts occur in it?

K: Whether there are thoughts or not, nobody thinks. The essential point is that there isn't a thinker anymore. Perception is free and not bound to a personal perceiver.

Q: Is an extreme situation necessary to realize this?

K: When there's no tomorrow and no yesterday, the eternal Now opens up. This happens in extreme situations. Often, during an accident or a war, where there's a constant threat of death, consciousness detaches itself from the body and only observes what's happening. Imre Kertész hints at this in *Fate*, his Nobel Prize winning book. He describes moments in a concentration camp where he experienced happiness, peace in the confrontation with death, and freedom through the absence of a hopeful "I." "If there is fate, freedom is impossible," he says, "and if there is freedom, there is no fate."

Q: So in an extreme situation, you suddenly get rid of your fate and are free. Is this the awakening we're talking about?

K: No, whatever can wake up (even in the face of death) will go to sleep again. Of course, It now wants to be awake all the time. But this very desire for wakefulness sends it to sleep again. Once you have the orgasm, you want it again and again because it doesn't last. It's something artificial, brought about by an extreme situation, a drug, or an action. Thus, it's not natural. You want to have it again, so you have to start another war.

Q: An orgasm isn't natural?

K: It's produced. A situation that's produced by something else isn't free, but dependent. But your natural state doesn't depend on some kind of action. Activity exists only as long as there's an apparent "I" that needs to dissolve. Its goal is "I"-lessness, but that which you are doesn't need a goal. It doesn't have any necessity to reach where it already is. Each "I" that goes into "I"-lessness must again come out of it. Whatever goes, comes again, and whatever comes, goes. Whatever is released will again be imprisoned. Whatever wakes up goes to sleep again.

Q: But isn't the seed sown with the experience of awakening? And if it happens in war, doesn't the experiencer become a pacifist and cease to fight?

K: Perhaps he does something else. The longing for the state of "I"-lessness remains. The pacifist, too, wants to reach "I"-lessness, which he seeks by trying to fulfill a desire for peace and harmony. Soldiers and pacifists have a common longing for this blissful state in which there's no more "I," no separation, no boundary. It's their common goal of waging war.

Q: But there are culprits and victims, aren't there?

K: As long as you're there, they'll be there, too. Let's begin with the root. If you didn't exist as a person, wars would cease. There'd be no more victims and no six billion other people— only consciousness, which is what you are. Consciousness manifests as war, as culprits and victims. But because you exist as the principal witness, the concepts of war and peace also exists, along with those further concepts that support or oppose them.

Q: Is it all my fault?

K: With the "I"-idea, the warrior is born. Only through you does war exists.

I Don't See One Who Suffers

The ultimate medicine for all suffering is to point out that there's no sufferer.

Question: No matter how you express it, I still experience suffering.

Karl: Suffering is the experience of separate existence. But is there someone who suffers because of it? Was there ever one? Or is this also just the experience that there's an experiencer who suffers from an experience? Did that which you are ever suffer? Did the perception that you are ever suffer from this fictitious suffering person, whose suffering is a further fiction?

Q: Why is it fictitious?

K: Is there a sufferer?

Q: Of course! Even if my body, mind, and personality are just phenomena, millions of other human beings are imprisoned in a similar picture of themselves, and I'm part of it.

K: As long as you make this claim, your existence will appear to be real.

Q: Exactly! And I have the desire to ease suffering for myself and all the others.

K: As long as this is your reality and as long as these desires appear, they're exactly as they should be, and whoever says that something is wrong or is an illusion is himself an illusion.

Q: Does the enlightened mind have no more desire to ease suffering?

K: It doesn't see sufferers any longer. Since it has disappeared as a sufferer, other sufferers have disappeared, as well. If you cease to exist, the other six billion also cease to exist. Only the Self and its manifestation exist. No second person exists; there's only the one being, the Absolute, being itself.

Q: Then one can't have compassion for illusions?

K: One can, but it's illusory compassion!

Q: If an enlightened one recognizes that in their illusions people suffer brutality, or at least believe they do, doesn't he have the desire to help?

K: I have no idea.

Q: Where is the compassion in what you say?

K: Compassion is the source of all of this.

Q: But it has to manifest itself!

K: It does manifest itself—as war and peace, for example.

Q: As war?

K: It also manifests as body, mind, and every variation of consciousness.

Q: Compassion manifests itself as war? As suffering?

K: It doesn't differentiate between good and bad.

Q: I suppose that suffering could have a point, but I want to know how to release people from this state.

K: You can only release people from suffering by showing them what they are in reality, not by taking away their suffering. The ultimate medicine for all suffering is to point out that there's no sufferer.

Q: Well, you've got to have the strength and desire to listen to that message. I'm sure that someone who's racked with disease and who lies in the dirt with nothing to eat would really be grateful for this hint!

K: Perhaps that person experiences right now that love for existence is an illusion. Many people come to their essence in extreme situations, such as being totally bereft of love or being surrounded by pressure and tyranny. In extremity, all this dissolves. Deliverance dissolves the perception of what perception perceives.

Q: Surely, enough people die in extreme suffering without this realization.

K: How do you know?

Q: Perhaps I'm only afraid of it.
K: Now?

Q: It always comes to the same thing?
K: Is there a sufferer now?

Q: Yes, I'm sure. And if it's not here, then it's outside.
K: If necessary, it'll be in the next life.

Q: Or it's me, here. I do exist.
K: Yes, the "I am" is already the beginning of suffering. If the "I am" is your reality, something else always comes out of it: a concept of how reality has to be. Then you're an idea that manifests in more ideas. As long as this is what you are, there's sorrow, but in truth you're freedom. You're not the "I"-thought with its longing for something. You're not the reflection of that which is suffering. You're the source, which is complete freedom.

Q: And is that true for all others, as well?
K: What others?

Meditation

Existence meditates on itself. This is what you are—meditation

Question: What is meditation good for?
Karl: It's good for nothing. Meditation is what you are. You're the meditator, meditating on yourself by recognizing yourself at every moment. Existence meditates on itself. This is what you are—meditation.

Q: I'm talking about something that I do. I sit down and meditate for twenty minutes.
K: That isn't meditation. That's an idea of self-improvement through the attempt to control something. You hope to move through meditation into harmony and thus attain Self-realization. Paradoxically, you hope to bring something into harmony that's already in complete harmony. The idea that I have to harmonize something comes from an idea of separation, the idea of standing outside and knowing better. At the

bottom of this attempt is an "I" that wants to be a surrogate god who can improve creation. A starry-eyed idealist passes judgment on the world with this verdict: "It's bad; it could be better; it has to be improved—in fact, by me."

Every human being is such a starry-eyed idealist, a small god who knows how existence really ought to be. In this sense, meditation is among the repertoire of techniques for improving the world. As long as the "I"-idea rules, people can choose from among various religions, paths, practices, and meditation techniques to improve the self and the world.

Q: Meditation is simply something valuable to me.
K: Every meditator thinks that he can do something special for himself that would be spiritual, special, and worth much more than drinking coffee, but this "medi-tating" or " medi-tactic" is a technique to control something. It's nothing special. When you spread butter on a slice of bread, you control the butter, so it spreads evenly across the bread. You harmonize the bread by spreading the butter evenly across it.

Go ahead, do it, but don't worry about anything else because harmony is present in every moment, no matter how you apply the butter. Existence harmonizes itself all the time, with or without your help or effort. Meditation serves the same function as spreading butter on bread. Whether you do it or not, existence never deviates from its essential harmony.

Q: But I find this technique useful.
K: It's fruitless and unstable in itself. You nurse and nurse the patient, but he never gets well. That's because you can't make something healthier that's already absolutely healthy. Existence has never lacked anything.

Q: What if I think something in my life is worth improving?
K: I only offer to help you see. Do you define yourself as a little wretch, an "I"? Or are you that which you are? Clearly, the One makes you content, while the other, the little wretch, brings suffering. It arises because you take yourself seriously, and this seriousness gets heavier and heavier.

Look at it. Are you that which is infinite lightness and harmony, or the little wretch who believes it has to endure the world?

Q: Do I have a choice?
K: No, but seize it anyway!

Preparation for Awakening

*Longing for bliss has guided your every step.
And each step is a preparation for the last step,
which leads into nothing, the abyss, the
mystery.*

Question: Sometimes I let thoughts pass by like watching a
crowd of people. I call this meditation, and it helps me arrive
at a wonderfully relaxed state. Is this a preparation for
awakening?

Karl: All that exists is preparation for your Self. As soon as
you come into this world, you long for your Self. As long as
the idea of life is your reality, you long for something beyond
it, something not conditioned by space and time, which is a
life of freedom. This longing appears as soon as you open your
eyes. Longing for bliss has guided your every step. And each
step is a preparation for the last step, which leads into
nothing, the abyss, the mystery.

Q: But aren't there some steps that lead more directly
toward it?

K: Are there some steps and paths more special than others? No. Every step is a special step toward yourself; every breath is special until the "I" doesn't breathe anymore, but is being breathed. There are steps, but not special ones. Simply trust what you are because the longing will lead you, one way or the other, to the Self that knows how to find itself better than any teacher or anything else. There's no way to avoid it; you can't miss yourself!

Q: But isn't part of the process reading certain books or coming to you?
K: Don't think that any one thing is more valuable than another.

Q: Coming here and reading (spiritual) books happen because of the desire to find myself again, or to find the Self again.
K: The Self, as an aberration called the small "I," searches for that which it is in its totality. But it can't do anything because it never lost it-Self! You can only find something that was lost or undiscovered, and you can only remember something you've forgotten. But you didn't lose anything, and therefore you'll never find anything. You didn't forget anything, and that's why you don't have to remember anything. Each attempt within relative knowledge to get to absolute knowledge is nothing but a nice try. Whatever you do is wonderful, but it doesn't lead to anything.

Yet each step taken by the Self leads you inevitably to the Self! At some time, it will awaken and see that it—Self has never been lost. That's all. You won't find anything, but simply realize that the one who seeks will never find because it's the object of the search itself.

Is It Permitted to Practice Relaxation?

*The Self is eternal relaxation, which has
nothing to do with relative tension and
relaxation.*

Question: The stillness I experience in meditation is good
for me. Are you going to tell me that there's something wrong
with it?

Karl: Each step is right, since it leads you to yourself. You
can't miss yourself. No matter where you go, you'll meet only
yourself. You can meditate as much as you want, turn your
back on your teacher, move into an ashram and then leave it,
follow the teaching of an avatar, or break every rule that's
laid down. You can play God or the Devil. Whatever you do is
neither helpful nor unhelpful; it's all wonderful.

Q: Well, I'll continue to meditate.

K: I would never say to stop it. By all means, continue!
Whatever the body-mind-organism does is made exactly for
the sake of this experience. For this experience to be

possible, what happens has to happen. It's always absolutely right, even when it's wrong. If for twenty years you've done this and missed that, you've done exactly the right thing.

Q: Of course, I meditate because it helps me become quieter.
K: What you are can't become quieter than it is, and what appears to become quiet is just an idea. A thought imagines a movement towards quietness, but it doesn't matter. Be aware of what's untouched by anything. It's totally power-less, never has any intention, and doesn't need any change. Whatever needs change is a thought, an idea, a phantom.

Q: You mean meditation doesn't change anything?
K: A thought can change a thousand times. The phantom that can develop within consciousness may be as great as an avatar or a god with an elephant head, but it's still separate and alone. Because it suffers from loneliness, it searches, longs for something, and has the feeling that it needs to do something.

Q: Even without an elephant head, we can do something to relax, can't we?
K: Relaxation isn't better than tension. Whatever can become tense or relax isn't what you are. The Self is eternal relax-ation, which has nothing to do with relative tension and relaxation.

Q: From your enlightened point of view, this may be so. But from my standpoint, there are differences between tension and relaxation.
K: What you're describing is simply an aspect of perception.

Who is the experiencer? How can he be changed or influenced by what he experiences?

You think that I see from my point of view and you from yours, but both are one and the same. Who sees here and who sees there? What's the difference? The Self that sees from an apparently enlightened viewpoint sees just as well from eyes that are seemingly unenlightened. Both are what you are. What difference is there between us?

Q: I suspect that you speak from the truth and I don't.
K: Nothing I've said so far is the truth. You can't recognize, know, or speak the truth. And the truth doesn't need someone to recognize it as the truth.

Q: What a pity! Nevertheless, I still continue to meditate.
K: You can't do anything else because you are meditation.

From Disruption to Catastrophe

Anything that requires something special can't be it. What you are is simple and effortless.

Question: I see clearly that truth can't be realized by the "I." But in meditation, the "I" disappears and becomes the truth.

Karl: No. Since a human being is only an object of experience, how can an object become that which is the essence? The human being can't become what it already is. An icicle that melts is water, and always was water. It doesn't become water, but the water takes on a different form. Water remains water, even when it changes form. Existence is similar. As an icicle, you don't become the essence; you already are the essence. An icicle can't achieve anything, but that which you are can achieve everything and can take on any form. It's already everything, but you fallaciously believe that you're separate from It.

Pure consciousness takes on infinite forms yet always remains consciousness. But no form can ever become the consciousness that it consists of, but will always remain just a mirage. Realize that you are the "I am," which is this pure consciousness.

Then be even prior to this "I am" as the pure "I." And then, even without the "I," there's just perfection. But let's go one step at a time; let's start with the "I am"!

Q: You go ahead and we'll follow.

K: You can remain seated; you don't have to go anywhere! You can be in relativity that which is prior to the one who realizes, the realizing, and that which is realized. You can recognize that which comes and goes as fleeting; you can see the transient isn't what you are. It's *neti, neti*—neither this, nor that.

What appears disappears, but you're that within which everything appears and disappears. This is meditation for which no effort is needed. You don't have to make an effort to be what you are. Anything for which you need to make an effort can't be what you are. Anything that requires something special can't be it. What you are is simple and effortless.

Q: But I work and have to make an effort if I want to get something done.

K: That which you are never made an effort and never will. Everything happens on its own. Whatever makes an effort isn't you, but part of the appearance. That which you are has never done or not done anything. Everything always happened on its own. It's all self made, and when you realize that everything Self made comes and goes on its own, who, then, can make an effort? Who, then, has anything to do?

Q: I don't, apparently.

K: Only the Self can liberate itself. Nothing ruled by time can make the Self into what it already is. Since only the Self can awaken itself, you can't call that which simply exists by itself an awakening. No action or meditation can bring about what only the Self can do. Through the power of will, whatever is in time can't do anything to reach something. Yet every step happening in time always leads toward yourself. No body, however, has ever taken a step or moved a step forward. If responsibility lies anywhere, it's with the Self, who did it all by doing nothing. It always walks towards itself, and it can never miss.

Everything the Self does leads to itself, and there's nothing special required on your part. In other words, "meditation," which is supposed to bring us to the Self, has no more relevance than stuffing sandwiches or watching TV, which supposedly leads us away from the Self. Everything you do is precisely calculated to bring you to the Self. There are no specialists as far as the Self is concerned. In this respect, I also know no more than anyone else. I only know that I am and that there's existence. Everything else is speculation. Truly, I know no more than you.

Q: I'm bewildered.

K: Accept your bewilderment as a small, disruptive event. You'll have many small disruptions before the final catastrophe happens, when the Self realizes itself, and the "I" ceases to exist; in fact, it's never existed. Self-realization is a catastrophe for the "I" because it's annihilated. It's like nuclear fusion: All the separate parts cease to exist by reverting to that which is their essence. In the fire of this awareness, everything relative disappears. In this Self-awareness, no relative idea can survive. Everything relative burns, and every idea of separation or non-separation disappears.

Q: I think I'd like to wait a little longer.
K: Yes, but that's also not up to you.

Am I the Emptiness?

You thought you had to become what you are!

Question: In meditation, I get into a state of complete emptiness, and I know that this is what I am.

Karl: Is it what you want to be?

Q: It's what I am, isn't it?

K: You'd like to feel at home—if not in your family, town, country, or even this world, then in the emptiness. At least there you'd have some kind of home: "Ah, the emptiness! There I'm at home!"

Yet no matter how you define yourself, in the moment of definition, you separate yourself from something else. Thus, when you say, "I'm the emptiness," something else lurks behind the emptiness and nothingness. Something is lurking there—and will always be there—as long as you define yourself as something.

Q: I thought I had to become this emptiness, which is what I am.

K: You thought you had to become what you are! What you try to become *is* what you are. If you think, "This harmony feels so wonderful; to be one with everything must be what I am," or "This emptiness in which nothing can touch me must be my true state," then you're longing for a state. But that which you are is always there. It's not a state, an experience, or a feeling.

You don't need to long for this, nor do you have to become it. Self-realization doesn't depend on proper behavior or correct conduct. It doesn't depend on any condition, such as becoming or changing, nor on some event in time, such as life or death.

Q: It sounds like infinity. I can't imagine it.

K: You can't imagine what you are. Because you're infinite, you can't imagine yourself. Neither can anyone else. Nobody can imagine you.

The Concept that Dissolves All Other Concepts

Resignation to "I"-lessness is liberation, which arises when you realize that the idea of reaching yourself is just an idea.

Question: The "I"-idea is growing weaker within me. But without this idea, one can't live!

Karl: Does that which you are need a thought to live and to exist?

Q: That which I am . . .

K: Who needs the "I"-idea? If anyone, it's only the "I"-idea itself.

Q: Then we'll let it drop away.

K: You don't need to drop anything. Nothing needs to go, and nothing needs to come. After all, we don't call it Self-murder, but Self-realization. But what is Self-realization?

Q: It, too, is an idea, just a concept.

K: If we want to talk, we need to use concepts. In this case, we're using a concept that, according to Ramana, "dissolves all other concepts." What concept is this?

Q: Please tell me. I don't want to think anymore.
K: The thought doesn't want to think anymore because as long as it doesn't want to think, it can stay.

Q: Please explain what Ramana means.
K: He's referring to the technique of staying with the question "Who am I?" Since it's impossible to answer this question, you remain in the mystery of the eternal question mark; it's a state of openness in which you don't know. This openness annuls the "I"-idea and its history. The doer or owner disappears in the openness of this unanswerable question. Like a fire, it burns the personal history, and nothing remains or survives in this not knowing what you are.

Q: I can never have the answer because the question mark is eternal! This sounds like suffering to me.
K: Suffering comes into being because you think, "If I find the answer, suffering will end." In truth, you'll never find an answer, and therefore suffering will never end. But is there a sufferer here and now, or does a sufferer exist only because he has the hope that suffering may stop in the future?

Q: Yes, perhaps that's the case.
K: As long as there's someone raising his hopes, thinking that he could become blissfully happy through answering the question "Who am I?," that someone will suffer because this question will never be answered.

Q: It sounds terrible.

K: We sit here so I can tell you again and again that you can never answer this question. You will never know that which you are because it isn't an object of knowledge. Whether you accept this or not, it's the way it is!

Q: But isn't this hopeless?

K: Hopelessness is your nature. In hopelessness, there's no more "I." Resignation to "I"-lessness is liberation, which arises when you realize that the idea of reaching yourself is just an idea. What you really are can never reach itself because however far it stretches, it can never grasp something that was never lost. This something is always here, fully and completely. The question "Who am I?" merely points to this mystery. It's a signpost that tells you to be completely what you are.

Q: And why don't I sense this?

K: Because there's no self that you could sense. It's not an object, a feeling, or a thought. Therefore, you'll never sense yourself or make contact with yourself. You're unknowable, ungraspable, and untouchable. You can never be touched by something else. You're absolute within yourself, unborn and immortal.

Q: Will I never know what I am?

K: While we talk about freedom, you want an answer that isn't free. You want to cling to an answer. That way, you can know that you exist, which ensures that you'll live with fear as your constant companion. As long as there's a "you" that has a deep insight, an enlightening experience, or an experience of God, you'll have to take care never to lose it for the remainder of your existence. What an effort!

Q: This doesn't remove my basic problem.
K: So what?

Q: Please answer my question. Is it wrong to desire to know myself?
K: No, it's only conceited. You want to know God, but what could be more conceited and fraught with self-importance? Trying to know yourself, you lament, "Life is so serious, and so difficult!"

The Virus: "Who Am I?"

In this inferno, known as "the inner fire of
awareness," only awareness remains.

Question: Ramana recommended to ask oneself the
question "Who am I?" Does it lead anywhere?
Karl: The question is like root canal surgery. Once it gets to
work, it removes the root. You start by asking yourself, "Am
I what I think? Am I the image I have of myself?" This
actually means, "Am I the ideas regarding myself? Do I appear in the morning as the 'I'-idea, or am I prior to it? Where
does this idea appear from? Within what does it appear? To
whom does it actually appear? Who sees it? Isn't what I am
prior to all thoughts and fleeting phenomena? Can what I am
be touched by anything at all?"

Q: This is just heady stuff.
K: Yes, it begins in the head. The Self searches for itself with
the intellect, emotions, and all possible faculties. It begins in

the head but spreads like a virus, always arising from the infection of "Who am I?"

This question is meditation itself. You direct the question toward itself, and thus you question the meditator. Awareness directs itself towards itself, not toward an object, a mantra, the breath, or a picture. It directs itself directly to the questioner. What is now aware of itself? What is here?

When you totally concentrate on this question, all personal history is slowly but surely annihilated, since in this question no person can exist anymore. This question is like the stick that stirs up the fire of awareness and at some point burns itself up. The question causes the "I" to consume itself in the flames. But whether and when this happens nobody can decide, prevent, or accelerate, since it happens on its own.

Even the question arises on its own. Posing the question as an essential expression of your being arises spontaneously in a moment. Then all other questions disappear. Only this one single question remains, which is totally directed toward itself. You don't decide when it happens; at some point in your life, the question arises. When it poses itself unavoidably and becomes your sole focus, Self-concentration begins. Ego-centeredness, which normally focuses on the world to have a relationship with everything external, now turns inward toward itself and leaves the world outside. Attention no longer focuses on anything fleeting. All objects vanish in this total awareness of itself. In this inferno, known as "the inner fire of awareness," only awareness remains.

Q: Does this mean that the world becomes insignificant?
K: Awareness is the source, while the rest is fleeting. When you pose the question "Who am I?" you aim attention at the

questioner. What aims? What is attention? Awareness aims at awareness; wakefulness aims at wakefulness. But you recognize that whatever happens in this wakefulness is nothing more than fleeting shadows on a screen. You see that awareness has always been what it is from the time you were a baby, and nothing has changed since then. Awareness is the most intimate experience and the only thing you know. It exists without condition while everything else is conditioned.

Without awareness and that which is aware (which can never be known), there would be nothing to be aware of. As awareness, you must always be there first. Only afterward do situations and circumstances occur. Awareness is equally complete in deep sleep; even when there's nothing to be aware of, you realize that in this awareness your birth happened as well. In this awareness your body came, and it will go again. Awareness was prior to this and will be there afterward.

You realize that awareness is unborn, and every idea of birth and death appears within it. Awareness itself was never born and will never die. You are the eternally unborn, the immortal, the source itself.

Q: Are we all the same awareness?
K: Awareness isn't selective. It's the absolute space in which everything happens. From one standpoint, awareness happens in space; it's visual, conditioned, and relative. From another standpoint, it's holistic awareness, the absolute stage on which everything happens and is experienced from all possible angles. However, as formless awareness, it exists even prior to this panorama as God's eye, pure, without time and space. The present moment arises in this eternity as one pearl glittering amid the infinite pearls of consciousness.

Q: So there is uniqueness!

K: Each moment is unique. No moment exists twice, just as there are no two identical snowflakes. Existence expresses itself uniquely. That which expresses itself here as Karl expresses itself there as that which you are. The expression is infinitely diverse. But that which expresses itself is always that which is.

Q: And is awareness, too, always different?

K: Awareness doesn't know one or two, separate or not separate. Awareness here is not different from awareness there. God always looks into himself and observes himself in the infinite variety of his unfolding as an infinite range of points of view. The Self is always realized, but here the word "Self" is merely a pointer. Within selflessness there's no more Self left that could know a Self, but only the complete absence of any idea of being or not being.

Q: And all this results from my asking the harmless question "Who am I?"

K: No, all this disappears. And you especially disappear.

The Dark Night of the Soul

You realize that it's pointless to search among objects for happiness and fulfillment.

Question: Before the so-called "awakening," must one go through a "Dark Night of the Soul"?

Karl: Are you asking whether or can one have it easier? At first, you define yourself as an "I" with qualities and stories that you call your identity. This "I" exists in a world that appears independent of you. Within this world you begin your search for objects that offer you fulfillment and circumstances that bring happiness. You expend much effort as you keep searching and searching until you don't search anymore. At some time, the searching stops, not because you've searched so cleverly, but because it simply stops.

You realize that it's pointless to search among objects for happiness and fulfillment. You see that there's nothing to find. At this point, you feel an emptiness within you and within the world, which you may experience as depression.

In this state, in which nothing can help you, you turn around and see that which is prior to this world.

Q: And that's the breakthrough?
K: You have nothing to do with it; it's all about consciousness. In the beginning, consciousness is searching for itself in the world, the realm of objectivity. Then it realizes, "The world and its objects can't satisfy that which I am because they're not real, but only apparent." With this realization, consciousness becomes still, and in this stillness it becomes aware of itself as pure awareness. As there's only One without a second, interest in the world falls away.

Q: But unfortunately, I still have interest in the world.
K: You have no cause for regret. You can't bring about the complete resignation from all objectivity and from every search. You can't create or prevent the condition in which only awareness remains, which takes place when consciousness withdraws from the world and turns toward itself. It can only happen on its own.

Q: Basically, I realize there's nothing to get through my efforts. In meditation, I always notice that nothing's really needed.
K: If you gave up everything, it wouldn't help you. You have no guarantee that anything will happen through meditating or searching. Whatever you do won't give you any advantage. It will help if you realize completely that you can't gain any advantage either through doing or not doing.

Q: For once you give a valuable tip!

K: It's nice that I could provide you with this small advantage.

Fear and the Absence of Meaning

*Desirelessness creates the bliss, which you try
to repeat through desire.*

Question: My experience with satsang is sometimes
mystical or divine. But when I'm alone, I notice that I haven't
taken anything with me; I fear it's all meaningless.
Karl: Would you describe your experience?

Q: During satsang, I feel a physical energy that makes me
tipsy, as if I have divine intoxication. When I leave here, I
simply feel fear. It's as if I'm addicted to what happens in
satsang.
K: What you're describing is selfishness, an addiction to
yourself. Every addiction originates in selfishness, with or
without drugs. The Self is the goal; longing for the Self is the
root. As long as you're not completely what you are, as long
as you still have an idea of separation, this addiction will
continue.

During satsang, you have moments when your disturbances cease because the sense of separation is temporarily
suspended and you experience unity. As your awareness
subtly shifts, you're initiated into a feeling of unification.
Satsang opens a door to an indescribable openness where no
separate "I" can enter. Buddhists call this a Buddhafield, and
during the time you're in it, you experience "I"-lessness, which
fills you with divine bliss. It also creates addiction.
Desirelessness creates the bliss, which you try to repeat
through desire. Do you see how every desire to get there works
against itself? How can you become desireless? How can any
step lead to the spaceless and timeless?

Q: You tell me!
K: I'm as completely helpless as you are at this point. I can't
bring you any hope. The process will happen the way it has
to until it's completed, and perception is wholly disengaged
from the perceived. In this process, perception, which is
connected to the perceived, becomes disconnected. This will
happen only when perception knows by not knowing. Since
there isn't any knowledge that can be conveyed, or any steps
to follow, it simply sinks into itself.

Q: This strikes me as sinking into horror.
K: If you can accept the Now, you may sink into it without
horror, struggle, or resistance. You'll simply dissolve. When
this happens, the controller falls quiet for a while and sinks
into the unthinkable.

Do I Have to Go Through Hell?

As long as there's someone who wants to get from Hell to Heaven, who wants to escape altogether or to turn some situation into a better one, the "I" remains real.

Question: What is the significance of Jesus' descent into Hell prior to his resurrection?
Karl: For whom is the question?

Q: I'm asking in general.
K: Simply ask yourself what it means to you. The only thing that's relevant is what you are, not others, society, or all of humanity. In this regard, be completely selfish; accept nothing but what you are. What's crucial isn't the opinion of others, but what's happening to you in the here and now. It doesn't matter how many people accept you or share your opinions. Such numbers are irrelevant. What really matters is that you remain independent of outer agreement.

Q: In concrete terms, do I have to go through Hell to wake up?

K: There's nothing you have to do, yet you do everything.

Q: I want to walk a gentle path. I don't want to experience Hell.

K: God's will always happens. If you are what you are, everything happens because it comes out of you. But when you consider yourself an "I," nothing that you want will ever happen. Whatever you want in your essence is what's happening, never what you want as an "I."

Q: If my essence plans things differently from me, does it mean I can forget what I want?

K: It's said that the Devil created free will in order to dominate you. Free will is the idea that you exist as something separate, which is a diabolical idea. Only when you exist as something separate do free will, conscience, and responsibility come into play. Only then does all this Hellish magic exist.

Q: How do I get out of it?

K: You can't withdraw. The entire essence of the great Hindu epic, the *Mahabharata*, is acceptance of Hell, which is the complete acceptance of suffering. In this acceptance, every idea of Hell and Heaven disappears. But as long as there's someone who wants to get from Hell to Heaven, who wants to escape altogether or to turn some situation into a better one, the "I" remains real. And as long as the "I" is real, with its ideas of deliverance and its willpower, everything is Hell.

Q: But there is deliverance, isn't there?

K: As long as you desire release, you remain imprisoned. The desire to escape is the desire to avoid yourself, and that's impossible. Even if you kill yourself a hundred times, you're still there. You can't escape what you are; nobody can. I can only show you the complete hopelessness of this attempt. If you realize completely that you can't escape, that you can't even escape from the attempt to escape, that there can't be a way out because no one's in, then there's peace.

Q: Damn it!

K: Don't worry; it's only a play, and you are consciousness that plays every role, from the most famous star to the most humble laborer.

Q: Well, then, I can't complain.

K: You can do that, too!

Consciousness Is a Bitch

*When creation is gone, there are no more ideas
and meaning, but only freedom.*

Question: In the past I longed for awakening. Now I'm feeling like having a break, but it doesn't seem possible.

Karl: If nothing else can make you content, except that which you are, then an unconditioned will awakens that has nothing to do with your personal will. This completely impersonal will, which can't be derived from your personal history, has a logic that you can't grasp. When this greater power takes over, you simply don't know what's going on anymore. It's as if an animal gets the better of you. Consciousness is a bitch. You can't calculate or predict what happens to you because it follows no condition.

Q: It sounds mysterious.

K: You are the mystery. When that which seems to have been asleep awakens, one can speak of grace. Consciousness becomes aware of itself and no longer allows anything else to bring satisfaction. Now the focus is only on it-Self. Everything else becomes stale, gray, and meaningless. For a while you think, "What am I still doing here?" You feel depressed, even horrified!

Q: Does depression come inevitably?
K: By "depression" I mean that a vacuum appears, an inevitable emptiness. Depression occurs when this emptiness appears in a person. If nothing—no object, person, or thought—can make you happy anymore, life becomes completely meaningless. This kind of depression does inevitably happen.

Q: What about the feelings connected with it?
K: Feelings are energetic vibrations associated with thoughts. We can distinguish among different types of feelings, such as melancholy, sorrow, or depression. But essentially they're energetic vibrations in the body, or energy turned into form. They don't need to concern you.

Q: I imagined that awakening would be more pleasant.
K: When grace comes, most people try to run away from it! They don't expect it to be so merciless in its mercy, so relentless and overwhelming! Grace gives you nothing and takes everything away.

Q: Does life then have no more meaning?
K: The lack of meaning brings with it a freedom from all ideas. Every hope or meaning you give to the world creates it and makes it real. As soon as it "exists," you become dependent

on this creation and want to squeeze a little happiness from it. Your creation is like a rubber band that's stretched out for a long time, and then it spr ings back, at last released. When creation is gone, there are no more ideas and meaning, but only freedom.

Q: I'm sorry, but this is rather frightening to me.
K: When U. G. Krishnamurti came to Ramana, he asked, "Can't you give me what I am?" Ramana said, "Yes, but can you take it?" The truth is indeed always there; there's no moment when it's absent. But can you bear this easiness, this unbearable lightness of being?

Can you accept that it's not up to you to decide what's acceptable and what isn't? Are you ready to be free of all difference and to no longer differentiate between pleasant and unpleasant? Can you accept what is unacceptable—the eternal sorrow of duality—as an aspect of your realization? Can you bear eternity? Have you gone as far as you can never reach? Can you, who are unending duality, also stand everlasting loneliness?

Q: Let's wait and see!
K: Can you bear loneliness? Isn't everything you do an avoidance of loneliness? Because you have the idea that you can't survive totally alone, don't you need a second in order to exist? Or does nobody exist anymore in this loneliness, not even yourself? Who can bear this? Can you bear the thought of thoughtlessness, or does it terrify you?

Q: It does.
K: But you have no alternative except to accept everything.

You do it, too. Acceptance is already what you are, including the acceptance of non-acceptance. You are the essence of acceptance and non-acceptance, and thus absolute acceptance.

Awakening is often described as a change from identified to non-identified consciousness, but in both cases someone still identifies with these states. Thus, someone identifies with non-identified consciousness. But you're the emptiness of emptiness, the fullness of fullness. You stay what you are in, all circumstances. Neither form nor formless, you're prior to all these ideas. You're also not formless consciousness. You're that which consciousness is, but you're not consciousness.

Q: I give up.
K: Who could give up?

Resignation and Divine Accident

*For most people because the price is too high,
they're not prepared to pay it. It costs yourself,
the idea that you are, that you exist. It costs
your entire existence.*

Question: I turn in circles. Every time I think that I've
finally got it, it disappears again.
Karl: That's wonderful! That's the beauty of it; nobody can
have it or grasp it. Whatever you can have or grasp is an
object and is thus transitory. But you can't grasp what you
are. When you give up the idea that you can ever find
meaning, perfection suddenly reveals itself—but only in this
complete resignation.

You signed the subscription form for the attempt to find
yourself, and in your resignation this subscription gets
cancelled. As you step back from the idea that you'll ever find
yourself, you find you're in the heavenly state of unknowing,
a state of perfection that's free of any desire to know yourself.

Q: What happens when I give up completely?

K: You simply spit out that bite of the apple you took from the tree of knowledge in the Garden of Eden. Eating the apple signifies the desire to know yourself, which gives rise to the "I"-idea. By taking a bite of the apple, you seemingly separate yourself from yourself. You step out of yourself with the intention of knowing yourself. You then suffer from the idea of separation until the moment of resignation when you step back into yourself.

Q: And then I enter paradise?

K: Paradise is what you are. You are "para," which means prior to what seemingly is. You're no longer appearance, but what's real. You step out of the apparent knowing, where whatever you know only seemingly exists, and return to what doesn't appear to be, which is that in which everything occurs. Without knowing it, you're complete in your-Self.

Q: But I can't achieve it! Do I just stumble onto it at some point?

K: Yes. In India it's called "the Divine Accident," the moment when the idea of a separate you disappears. It's "divine" because this accident happens spontaneously; you can't influence it. If you could, everyone would urgently need to learn how to create an accident. But in fact, teachers try to help you avoid it. They say, "Careful, there's a tree over there, so please go round it. Don't head directly toward it!" Then crash, bang! You have the Divine Accident; you collide with infinity, and the ego bursts!

Q: But it costs something.

K: It costs you everything. For most people, because the price is too high, they're not prepared to pay it. It costs yourself, the idea that you are, that you exist. It costs your entire existence.

Q: Then I shouldn't be after recognition anymore?
K: There shouldn't be anybody who's after recognition.

Q: One could spit at me or humiliate me . . .
K: But there's nobody left, so who cares?

Q: I see. But how does it feel, then, not to exist anymore?
K: Forget about how and why and what for. Forget about time, too. Only in time do you exist; when there's no more time, you don't exist.

Q: I can't imagine that.
K: Because you want to imagine it, time exists.

Q: When I hear that it costs everything and nothing of the self remains, I find the price is really too high.
K: Of course! You'll never be ready to pay the price. That's why grace is necessary: The Self wins the lottery, takes you as the prize, and you disappear. You are a lottery ticket, and at some time your number will be drawn, which means your separate self will vanish.

Q: But if I . . .
K: No, there's no chance of doing anything. The Self always wins.

There Never Was a Happy One

You are the source of time. Every morning when you open your eyes, you create this world. The body wakes up, not you. The wakefulness that you are is already there. It never slept.

Question: Sometimes I have the impression that there's only unhappiness in the world.
Karl: Who has this impression?

Q: I do. It makes me depressed.
K: Be what you are, and you'll always feel fine. In the absence of an "I," there's nobody left who could feel bad. One who's happy is always driven to become unhappy. Relative happiness always drives you again to unhappiness. The relative happiness of this world is synonymous with unhappiness. There is only unhappiness in this world! You're right.

Q: That's hardly consoling.
K: That's why Jesus didn't say, "I came to bring peace and love into the world." Instead, he said the opposite: "I came

not to bring peace, but a sword." This statement means, "The world can't make you happy. There's no peace in this world, but only unhappiness. No one has ever been happy in this world."

Q: Stop it!

K: People always asked Jesus why, as the son of God, he couldn't rule and bring eternal happiness by making the earth a paradise. Why didn't he have the omnipotence of God? He answered, "Let the dead bury the dead." This means that the world is dead. Who cares what it looks like? Let the dead be busy with the dead. The world is nothing but a phenomenon, an idea you have that's no more alive than a dream or a nightmare, which seems real only so long as no one pinches your toe. Then you realize, "This terrible persecutor or this infinite chasm into which I just fell screaming isn't real at all!" No, it wasn't real and it isn't real. Real is what you are, and its happiness doesn't depend on a dream.

Q: But I am, after all, a child of this time and can't deny . . .

K: No, you're not a child of this time. Time is a child of yours! You are the source of time. Every morning when you open your eyes, you create this world. The body wakes up, not you. The wakefulness that you are is already there. It never slept.

Be this wakefulness. In any event, it's what you are. You're prior to the "I" and the world, but you believe in your intellect. You're fascinated by this world, which the intellect projects, and you immediately want to improve it. This desire makes you unhappy, so you start your search for happiness.

Q: How and when do I find it?

K: You have an appointment with yourself, which you can't miss. When will you keep this appointment? When you don't create time anymore. How will you keep the appointment? You keep it by stopping all efforts to find happiness in external objects.

You won't find happiness in your projection of the world, but much more simply in being what you are. Whether you call it Christ nature or Buddha nature, it's what you are. You are unborn and immortal; your nature is bliss.

The Painful Idea of Life

The pain stops with the realization that you're nothing that can be separate from anything else.

Question: I've heard of immortal avatars in the Himalayas. Aren't there yogis who attained immortality?
Karl: What would be gained by that, and who would gain it? Death is just another experience within the infinity of experiences. When and how it comes doesn't matter. That which experiences is always existence, which remains untouched by any "death experience."

Q: That's nice for existence, but I think more of myself.
K: You have no existence as a separate being. It's only an idea.

Q: Actually, I rather like the idea.
K: Death, birth, and everything in between are self-experiences that occur within a personal history. However,

existence itself perceives every personal history, which means that no separate being experiences or perceives anything. Only awareness perceives at every moment. That which speaks here also listens over there; neither is separate.

Q: Then my great grandfather and I aren't separate, either. But something tells me that he's dead and I'm alive.
K: At this moment, is there the thought of life?

Q: Yes, if you want to express it that way.
K: Where's this thought of life when you sleep deeply?

Q: Of course, it's not there.
K: That's death, which is the absence of the idea of life. In death it's all finished! Both life and death are ideas. The idea of life can exist only where there's also the idea of death.

Q: According to this idea, is there anything left of me?
K: That which remains is what you are, which is equally present in deep sleep when such ideas are absent. What now appears so real to you is in truth unstable and fleeting. However, that which you truly are can't come and go. It's present in all states. Deep sleep is a state of emptiness in which nobody perceives anymore. Yet that which you are is as present then as now.

Q: Is it equally possible that I died and that I merely believe . . .
K: Yes, that could be. I can only tell you that to live in the "I"-idea is truly death. It's death through suicide, which literally means "self-killing." In the "I"-thought, which is the idea of

separation, that which you are is dead. By believing in this thought, you leave the perfection of being, which is your natural state, and enter into something unnatural, which is separation.

Q: And yet this "I"-idea is dear and precious to me.

K: It's precious because it's based on ignorance of your true nature, and this hurts. The pain stops with the realization that you're nothing that can be separate from anything else. With this realization, nobody has any pain, and nobody has any experiences, including pain. You're prior to the one who experiences. But as long as you turn yourself into a reflection, you experience suffering.

Q: Do I understand you correctly that as long as I believe that I exist, it will hurt?

K: You'll hurt as long as you experience yourself as separate from pain and want to avoid it. The avoidance itself is pain. Be that which is pain and that which is existence. Then it's no longer pain, but a vibration within you, an experience of what you are. You're the essence of pain.

You're the existence within which the sensation of pain appears. Be this and see what happens. Does anyone have this pain? At this moment, no one owns it, so you no longer need to turn it into your story.

Q: Perhaps I'm attached to pain because it gives me the feeling that it's me who lives.

K: Then you don't live. Death truly occurs at the moment when you think you live. As long as you think you're in this world, you're in a state of death.

Q: Then why are there six billion people who think that they and the world exist?

K: It's the other way around: As long as you think that you exist, there are six billion people.

Q: What's all this for?

K: The Self, which created a scientific experiment for itself called "consciousness in search of itself," and put you into a test tube.

Q: Now we'll have some fun.

K: Yes, because now it's looking for a Bunsen burner!

How Does One Die Properly?

I'm not interested in the thinker, the "I"-idea,
which can't keep up with these words. I don't
even see it. I don't speak to any person here.

Question: Does it matter whether one dies consciously or in delusion?
Karl: No.

Q: But almost all religions teach that how one dies is important.
K: Oh, you know about this?

Q: I don't, but many enlightened beings say that the time of death is relevant.
K: Do you want to question God or existence?

Q: Excuse me?
K: Do you want to say that consciousness is stupid and doesn't know what it's doing?

Q: I really don't believe in the stupidity of God.
K: Does God know what he does?

Q: I certainly think so.
K: But you think we have to take care whether a being dies this way or that way. Or is it possible that God knows better?

Q: God may know, but still it's important that we do something.
K: Do we need to improve the world?

Q: I don't think that indifference is the answer.
K: Doesn't one who improves the world place himself outside the whole as a separate god?

Q: Isn't there a difference between someone with grand ideas of improving the world and someone who just wants to lend a hand?
K: Perhaps not a big one. If you want to help someone else, you want to change what is. I don't say it's wrong. But as long as there's someone who thinks an improvement is necessary, and as long as it's real for him, he's suffering. Pity for someone else comes from self-pity.

Q: I'm talking about compassion.
K: Nobody can have compassion. In compassion, you don't exist anymore.

Q: But the others are still there.
K: In compassion, the others don't exist either.

Q: That means compassion can manifest in this body! Perhaps then it will want to do something.

K: Compassion, which is your essence, doesn't differentiate between good and bad experiences. It doesn't sympathize with pain-free or pain-full experiences. In compassion, pain, too, is an experience of Self-realization. Since its only quality is perception, the Self realizes itself in everything. There's only the compassion of the Self for the phenomenal world.

Q: Stop it! Stop this bombardment of logical connections. The way you communicate this is too much for me.

K: I don't want to communicate anything. I intend that what I'm saying is "too much."

Q: Well, you've succeeded with this deluge of intellectual concepts.

K: You have a concept of compassion, which is the idea of personal pity. I oppose it with the principle of the Self.

Q: Yes, but why go about beating us up intellectually, rather than touching us? Don't you want to touch us?

K: No, I don't want to touch anybody.

Q: If I'm not touched, what you say passes me by.

K: It's supposed to pass you by because then something else listens. Consciousness is talking here, and consciousness is listening there. I'm not interested in the thinker, the "I"-idea, which can't keep up with these words. I don't even see it. I don't speak to any person here.

Q: Well, then, have fun.

K: The only thing that can happen is the acceptance that you have a concept and I have a concept. Acceptance brings forth everything. Compassion, which accepts the entire cosmic existence, creates the words that consciousness is speaking here and hearing there as a flow of energy. It doesn't matter what we're talking about. Neither does it matter whether we come to a result or have a realization.

Q: What happens in space without words is important to me, yet I feel that you fill the entire space with words.
K: It sounds good.

Q: You talk fast and use certain terms as you connect ideas with them. But first of all, I need to get a feeling of what these mean. My intellect has to keep up. Look, doesn't what happens here have any importance? It matters to me.
K: Who's now saying what's important?

Q: I am!
K: Who's "I"?

Q: For heaven's sake, I simply want to know how one dies and whether one can do anything!
K: You're dying right now, so take a look at yourself.

Q: I see only dissolution.
K: And can you do something?

Q: I don't know anymore.
K: Good.

Q: Yes, very good.

K: That's why I'm called Karl-Schlag (a pun on the German *Kahlschlag*, meaning demolition).

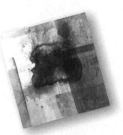

Does an Enlightened Being Continue a Normal Life?

The absolute is my nature, and the personal situation in which I appear to be, as a part of this world, doesn't matter at all.

Question: Can anyone describe what enlightenment is?

Karl: We can talk only about what's accessible to thinking and language. But where the Absolute is concerned we can give only the hint that it's beyond all definition. As Lao-Tsu said, "The Tao one can name isn't the eternal Tao." The only way to remove all doubts about this is to become aware of one's absolute nature.

Q: Is this your feeling of being alive?

K: It's the feeling of the aliveness that's absolute, not relative.

Q: Right now, do you have the feeling of absolute aliveness?

K: Nobody can own it.

Q: What a pity!

K: It's your nature. You don't need to do anything to be yourself. It's what you are completely, here and now. At this moment, you're directing your attention toward something fleeting. Because you have the feeling that it's real, the fleeting becomes reality for you. If you directed your attention toward that which always exists, the absolute would be your reality. It would be the only living thing, since there's no other life!

When you direct your attention toward what's permanent, you recognize while living in the world that what you are is no longer part of the world. You recognize what you are while still in the body, but you're no longer the body.

Q: It must be a strange feeling.

K: About two thousand years ago, someone said, "My kingdom is not of this world." This doesn't mean that the kingdom is up in the sky and that if you do the right thing, you'll get there some time. It means that my kingdom has nothing to do with any kind of imagination. It has nothing to do with what you believe you see. The Absolute is my nature, and the personal situation in which I appear to be, as a part of this world, doesn't matter at all.

Q: No matter what happens?

K: No matter whether I'm hanging on a cross or going out with Mary Magdalene. These are just circumstances, mere appearances. They have nothing to do with what I am. Jesus even says, "I am that which is God, but I am not God." This means that he is the essence of God, that which is knowledge without having to know anything. In this absolute knowledge, no one is there who knows—or needs to know—anything. No one is there who cares whether he's alive or not. To point toward your essence, all we can say is that it's the absence of any idea of whether you exist or not.

Q: I'm getting dizzy. Does this feeling of being alive mean that whatever happens to us is all the same?
K: There's nothing left that could happen to anything. In the fleetingness of a shadow world, consciousness behaves actively and reactively. You're not part of the phenomena in the shadow world, but always prior to them. In reality, nothing moves; there's only pure stillness.

Q: But here we're moving and talking. I'm still aware of an "I" that participates—or at least acts as if it does!
K: The "I" continues as before without any difference.

Q: Does the "I" experience that whatever happens is all the same?
K: For Little Karl, what happens isn't irrelevant. Little Karl has intentions and wants this or that. The only possibility for him is complete acceptance, whether or not he gets what he wants. Whether or not he dies in the next moment makes no difference. Every night, when Little Karl goes to bed and disappears, the attitude is "In case I don't see you again, it was nice having met you!" and every morning around eight, it's "Oh God, it's you again!"

Q: What if something nastier happens?
K: It can only happen to what you are. If something kills you, you only kill yourself, and thus nothing can be killed. If the

body dies, it's killed by the consciousness playing this body. The appearance of the body may vanish, but your immortal existence hasn't lost a thing.

Immortality

Nobody's born or dies. Ultimately, death brings this realization, which is why it's liberating.

Question: Is death the end?

Karl: Yes, it's the end of body, mind, and soul; most of all, it's the end of all you ever thought you owned. You thought various things belonged to you, such as material possessions, "your" character traits, and the soul (at least a bit of it). But none of them remains. The owner dies—the owner of car, house, and garden; children and family; body and feeling; mind and soul. The owner of experiences, the owner of a history, dies irrevocably. Then comes something like a zero point, followed by complete freedom, in which you look into that which is and accept whatever happens unconditionally. In this final understanding, you realize that nothing belongs to you, which brings freedom.

Q: Does freedom come only with death, or can it exist earlier?

K: At every moment, you should die—or at least confront death and your mortality. Whatever you meet, own, experience, or want to hold on to is mortal and fleeting. Whatever you gain you'll lose. You'll even lose the "I," the idea of your separate self. In the face of mortality, the idea of ownership disappears: "My body, my life, my karma, and my history" are all over. In the face of mortality, every "my," the owner of experience, disappears. And yet you remain completely present as what you are.

Q: What part of me remains?

K: You remain as that which is prior to the idea of ownership and mortality. Your essence isn't touched by anything fleeting, by the idea that you've owned or can lose anything, which are merely ideas. In truth, you're always free, always in the eternal Now where no personal history exists. Thus, nobody's born or dies. Ultimately, death brings this realization, which is why it's liberating.

Q: I've always thought that when we die, we become light.

K: In death everything loses its heaviness. Nothing remains that needs to be carried; in fact, nobody exists anymore who could carry anything. Therefore, let die what can die and see what you are. Even now, as the gravestone looms menacingly before you, what's still completely present? When your body is buried and all your memories and experiences are gone, what still exists? What exists now? Perhaps you already live in the cemetery and just think you're alive! Perhaps everything you see is dead already, and whatever you experience dies at the same moment it's born. Whatever comes and goes is dead, while the only thing alive is you.

Q: That doesn't help me. My father is about to die, and soon we'll clean out his apartment. We'll throw his books, letters, and dreams into the trash container.

K: All ideas connected to life are blown away in the face of emptiness.

Q: Yes, emptiness remains, but that doesn't give me consolation.

K: Emptiness means the absence of an "I," yet something is completely present in this emptiness. This something is you and your father, both complete even in emptiness.

Emptiness means the absence of everything except what you are. You exist as something indescribable, indefinable, ungraspable, yet completely present in this emptiness and untouched by it. Death is just a circumstance that can't touch, influence, or change what you and your father are.

Q: I've been present when people died, and because tremendous fear was present, their transitions weren't always joyful.

K: That's completely natural. As a result of the survival instinct, the one who believes it will die experiences fear. There's nothing wrong with this. However, at the moment of death, when the fight for survival ceases, there's only clarity. Struggle and fear come to an end. In the absence of forms and ideas, everything is simple and clear.

Until this moment, struggle, fear, and resistance have every possibility of manifesting. But when the final, the ultimate, dawns, there's nobody left who can fight; there's simply emptiness by itself. In it this awareness, which is here now but seems to be concealed, is denuded of desires, ideas, and concepts. This emptiness is complete existence; it's completely clear and pure.

Q: Existence remains, but I'm dead.
K: What is alive, anyway? Can life be mortal and therefore subjugated by death? In truth, whatever can die is already dead beforehand; it never lived and thus can't die. There's nothing in the moment of death that can die. You are pure existence. It's here and now, the only thing that is, and at the moment of death, it's still the only thing that is.

Q: You speak of existence, but unfortunately, that's not what I am.
K: Even if you say, "It's not me," it doesn't matter. Your denial doesn't change or diminish your nature. You remain completely what you are, which needs no proof. The "I" always lacks evidence of the Self. The "I" uses all the means at its disposal to continue the search for meaning. Without the desire for meaning, it would be finished. But even with all its struggles, death finishes it anyway. Death makes it irrelevant.

In death, all questions of "Why?" "How?" or "What for?" suddenly disappear. In the face of emptiness and timelessness, the "I" and all its questions are superfluous.

Q: But that's exactly what I'm afraid of.
K: As the greatest advisor in your life, death confronts you with the mortality of your body, mind, and soul. Death means the end of all you believed yourself to be. In the face of death, you have to question the belief that this concept of an "I" really exists. I advise you to question it now.

Q: That's what I'm doing.

K: If death can't touch you, what was born and who dies? If death can't touch you, were you ever born?

Q: Up until now, I always assumed I was.

K: The ideas of birth and death are fleeting thoughts in the world of your experiences. You're that which is eternally untouchable, which never came and never will go.

Pointers

These are pointers to that which doesn't require cognition or enlightenment to be what is. And this is what you are: Absolute Being in imperturbable harmony.

Everything is exactly the way it is because Being has manifested itself this way and not otherwise.

The first idea of "I" falsely conditions everything that follows it. Therefore, only the absolute cognition of being prior to the "I"-thought and the recognition of the false as false will remove the root of all problems.

By being what you are, or better, *as* you are—absolute, prior to all, and nothing—all concepts are destroyed.

Your true nature is eternal, *prior* to the appearance of time, space, and all that arises in it. Eternally untouched, this absolute awareness perceives itself in and as itself.

∞

Recognizing the ego as a fleeting shadow in the eternal Now voids its apparent reality.

∞

Is there ever a moment in time when the Self is not realized? That which you think you are will never be realized. How can an idea or an object be realized? Realization means that consciousness, which was once identified with an object, becomes infinite; it becomes conscious about being consciousness.

∞

The Self is never enlightened or unenlightened. It is always *prior* to all ideas of enlightenment or non-enlightenment, no matter what you say about it, which is just conceptual.

∞

The only thing that isn't conceptual is the Self. With concepts you can look at things from infinite angles and in the process make new and different concepts. Seeing doesn't require an explanation! It requires pointing to the very core and seeing that only the Self is reality, which is *prior* to all ideas of existence or nonexistence. Any idea that arises is fiction. That which is *prior* to fiction, to ideas, is what you are.

∞

Replacing one concept with another concept in order to create a "clear" concept doesn't give an advantage at all. This is not part of understanding. We are speaking of what you *are*, which doesn't require understanding or knowledge of how it functions.

∞

"No one" ever realized anything, not even Karl, who is part of the realization. Even though you're full of desire to improve or change, really *see* that there is not now, nor will there ever be, a way out of what you are. You can never become what you already are!

∞

Awakening isn't something that "happens"; it's just an "aha"— seeing that what you are is what you always were and always will be. What you are is outside of time. Time exists because of you; it's merely a partial reflection of yourself.

∞

There never was an ego that breathed. There is no "last" breath because there was no "first" breath. Don't create a process out of it; there's no process. Just see that what you are is the only real thing and that it was never touched by whatever is sensorial. This is not something new; it's ancient and infinite. Just this—"aha, oh, infinity"—and all there is is the infinite, not an experience or an event.

∞

Out of the idea of an "owner" comes the idea of owning consciousness. This happens because of the feeling of separation. What results is the sense of being a separate person, which is also false. Consciousness plays the role of a person, but there's no person who "owns" consciousness. If there is any ownership at all, it's on the part of consciousness, which "owns" a person, since it plays the role of that person.

∞

The only possible death is the death of the ego (the idea of separation). And the question is, how can something die that doesn't exist? How can something die that is an appearance and that presents itself in perception only as sensation? By what can the lie of being separate disappear? For *what* or for *whom* does the lie of separation disappear?

∞

There's no creator and no creation. There's only the one Self and its unfolding, which is infinite. Because there's nothing outside the Self, there can't be a separate creator or creation. Out of this unfolding, the "I" as awareness becomes the thought "I am"; from the thought "I am" comes the feeling "I am an object in time." All this takes place as part of the Self's unfolding.

Ramana Maharshi said that just as you use one thorn to remove another lodged thorn, you use one concept to remove another concept, after which both are discarded. Similarly, all this investigation helps you realize that you're nothing conceptual. You see this absolute experience when you're in total emptiness and there's no "second."

When there's nothing to perceive, you remain as you are. In this total emptiness, we can't say whether you are or you are not. Thus you exist without an idea or perception of anything. You remain what you are, even when the sensation of being "you" no longer exists.

When you see that nothing has ever happened, there are no more steps. You are what you always have been and always will be; the rest is just *lila*—a theatrical play.

The Self doesn't depend on anything, nor is it the caretaker of what unfolds. The Self, which is as it is, is perfect in itself. The absence of all ideas of what the Self is or is not brings perfect happiness and contentment.

Always come back to the following point: Be *prior* to that which exists in time. See that what you are can't be perceived through any of the senses.

In its Omnipresence, the Self reveals itself in its Omnipresence, in the eternal Now. A disciple co-appears with a teacher like a question with its answer. Out of desirelessness, a desire arises in time and dissolves itself in its fulfilment, just as every question finds redemption through an answer. This is the karmic law of consciousness. There is neither teacher nor student, only questions and answers.

The unfolding of the Absolute is as absolute as that which is unfolding. Even this image called "me," which pops up in the morning and goes down in the evening, is without any need of realization. As long as you believe you're this image, as long as this "I"-thought is your reality, the Self is only an idea. It's consciousness looking for the Self.

Only the Self looks. It doesn't matter how the Self looks: from in time, out of time, or prior to time. The Self perceives, and what it perceives is only the Self, since the Self is all there is.

⚭

You may call the Self the source of the "I am," which is the source of "I am Karl," but you can truly rest only when you see that whatever you define can't be what you are. Just as the eye can't see itself, the absolute definer can't define what the definer is. What you are can't avoid resting in "what is," nor can it rest in something else because Self is all there is.

⚭

You can't escape because all there is is the Self. Wherever you may go, you will already be present. Whether you stay still or move about, no one moves and no one stays still. Just see the totality of what you are, even in the world of time and space. This totality is all there is.

⚭

Awareness is the first unfolding; it's a sense of self that's aware of existence. Thus there's a self aware of its separateness. In this way, awareness is already part of separation.

Time comes out of the idea of a "me." All these ideas are only part of the unfolding of the totality, the Self. Even though you may perceive what seems to be finite time, which appears to come and go, it doesn't mean that it exists finitely.

∞

No work or development is required for being what you are. All concepts of a "way," which involve development and even cognition, appear with the first "I"-thought. This first idea creates time, space, and thus the entire universe.

∞

As long as this "I"-thought appears to be real—which means separation, two-ness, and suffering—the desire for unity appears, along with the longing for a way out and for an end to suffering.

∞

Look for the *beginning* of suffering. When you can find the beginning, then you may find the end, as well. Did suffering ever start? For suffering to be present, there must be a sufferer, so look for the sufferer first. As long as you look for the "end" of suffering, there will continue to be a sufferer.

∞

The sense of "I am" brings with it a sufferer—maybe not suffering—but at any moment, without attention, it can go back to suffering. When you annihilate the idea of a sufferer, where is the suffering?

∽

The total annihilation of the sufferer can take place only when you really see what you are—when you perceive yourself without beginning and without end. When you see this manifestation only as the Self, there is absolute annihilation of the sense of separation and existence as a separate self.

∽

Don't listen to anybody, not even to yourself. Whatever you perceive can't be what you are. Whatever you've understood you can forget. What can disappear can surely appear again.

∽

The ego that goes may return sooner or later. First, see what actually appears and whether that appearance is real. Then who cares about an appearance? This is the main question to ask, not what comes and goes. How stupid to care about an appearance. Ignorance of the Self, the belief in a separate self, takes an appearance as real.

Most spirituality is just "Dharma-keeping." It keeps the Dharma alive; it keeps the *lila* alive.

叐

Recognize everything as a lie, especially the one who recognizes everything to be a lie.

叐

The ideas that "I am without form" or "I am not" are still within the realm of separation. "Who" has no form but still needs one? Just see that what exists in "no form" exists in form also. I'm the same either with or without form. Without the sense of difference, without the sense of separation, it's all complete.

叐

You don't require any special circumstance. What you are exists in any and every circumstance. The circumstances we call birth or death can never touch you. You are *prior* to the sensation of birth and death. What you are existed before this body was born.

叐

See that you are total compassion, that nothing happens to you, that whatever arises is because you are. There's no difference between this eye looking at something or the other eye; you are the infinite eye, which looks from infinite angles into what you are. You are the infinite perception, which perceives only Self-information.

∞

The main thing to see is that there's no need for a way out. And in this resignation—the realization that you're the essence or substratum of what is—there's no way out because you *are* the very source of what is. Only then is there peace.

∞

Do you see the fruitless ping-pong play of concept against concept? The only problem is that there are concepts. This conceptualization hides the Truth.

∞

To see the Emptiness of concepts is to see their essence, which is Freedom. And in this seeing even the seer disappears.

∞

Emptiness, your absence, is like a snake: If taken properly, its poison can cure; if used improperly, its poison can kill.

∞

The absence of any separate sense of "you" and "me" is the ultimate medicine. When this is understood through the filter of the mind, the master of all concepts, the world is full of suffering and death. When this is understood by the Heart, there's no separation. You're one with all suffering, including the suffering of the child in Ethiopia, but with this difference: There's an absence of a personal sufferer.

❦

To approach Reality, words are useless. Only the deep silence of stillness enables all the objects of the world, including you and me, to disappear into the awareness of total potentiality, into everything, into *I Am That I Am.*

❦

In the absence of a "you," there's no longer any judgment, so if helping "others" is to take place, it's not in "your" hands.

❦

There's no "you" to achieve a goal, since there can be no individual in this Absence. Here, where every action or nonaction is absolute, there's no sense of doership. Everything happens spontaneously and completely naturally.

❦

When the Heart is covered by the sense of your own individuality, the world appears as a separate Hell. When this sense of separation is gone and the heart is uncovered, Emptiness, our true home, appears as Paradise. That's what *para* (before and after all appearances) means. It will only and always be the Absolute.

Just see! The Self is all, and whatever takes place is only in and of the Self.

There's nothing more to say when Emptiness *is*.

About the Author

Karl Renz holds dialogues and meetings throughout the world. You may find his schedule and additional information at: www.KarlRenz.com

About Inner Directions

Inner Directions is the imprint of the Inner Directions Foundation, a nonprofit organization dedicated to exploring self-discovery and awakening to one's essential nature.

We publish distinctive books, videos, and audiotapes that express the heart of authentic spirituality. Each of our titles presents an original perspective, with a clarity and insight that can only come from the experience of ultimate reality. These unique publications communicate the immediacy of *That* which is eternal and infinite within us: the nondualistic ground from which religions and spiritual traditions arise.

If you recognize the merit of an organization whose sole purpose is to disseminate works of enduring spiritual value, please consider becoming a financial supporter. To find out how you can help sponsor an upcoming publishing project, or to request a copy of the *Inner Directions Journal/Catalog*, call, write, or e-mail:

Inner Directions
P. O. Box 130070
Carlsbad, CA 92013

Tel: 760 599-4075
Fax: 760 599-4076
Orders: 800 545-9118

E-mail: mail@InnerDirections.org
Website: www.InnerDirections.org